SARAH'S SONG

A
TRUE STORY
of
LOVE AND COURAGE

JANICE A. BURNS

WARNER BOOKS

A Time Warner Company

Grateful acknowledgment is given for quotations from the following:
Jane Eyre by Charlotte Brontë. Copyright © 1982, New York: New American Library.
"On Virginity" by John Chrysostom, in *Women in the Early Church*, edited by Elizabeth A. Clark. Copyright © 1983, Wilmington, DE: Michael Glazier, Inc.

WARNER BOOKS EDITION

Cover design by Rachel McClain

Warner Books, Inc.
1271 Avenue of the Americas
New York, NY 10020

Visit our web site at
http://pathfinder.com/twep

 A Time Warner Company

Printed in the United States of America

Originally Published in Hardcover by Warner Books.
First Paperback Printing: September, 1996

10 9 8 7 6 5 4 3 2 1

PRAISE FOR *SARAH'S SONG*

"BURNS'S PROSE IS AS LYRICAL AND POETIC AS THAT OF THE BEST AUTHORS YOU COULD NAME. The story she has to tell is riveting and tragic, but not once does it come off as pitiful. At its core, it's a love story . . . one of the most bittersweet you'll ever read. There is no better purpose for a book than to change people's lives. This one has changed mine."

—*Willamette Week* (OR)

"NEVER BEFORE HAVE I CRIED THE WAY I DID AS I CONCLUDED SARAH'S SONG. Janice Burns has crafted one of the most powerful, gut-wrenching books I've ever read."

—Andrew Strickman, *Inlander Supplement*

"IT IS A STORY OF LOVE, DEVOTION, AND COURAGE, THE LIKE OF WHICH WE RARELY SEE. . . . IT IS SHEER POETRY."

—Fr. Robert Warren, SA, AIDS Ministry

"THE COUPLE'S GREAT DEVOTION TO EACH OTHER AND THE AUTHOR'S STRENGTH ARE EVIDENT."

—*Library Journal*

"JANICE BURNS GIVES US A BOOK THAT TEACHES A GREAT DEAL ABOUT FAMILY, GRACE, AND ABOUT COURAGE. Most of all, though, it teaches about the great power of love. This is a gift that should not be refused."

—Mark S. Rapoport, M.D., M.P.H.,
Commissioner of Health, Westchester County, New York

O   O   O   O   O   O

JANICE A. BURNS and her husband coauthored *HIV in Putnam County: Profile of a Growing Epidemic*. Widowed in 1994, Ms. Burns is currently vice-chair of the Westchester AIDS Council. She has written for *Body Positive* magazine, and she is a founding member of *Living Together*, an advocacy group for people affected by HIV in Westchester, Putnam, and Rockland (NY) counties.

In memory of my husband, Bill,
whose love gave me the courage to live

Acknowledgments

Sarah's Song could not have been completed without the help and support of the following people:

All the members of my family, especially my parents, Joan and John O'Reilly, whose unconditional love and acceptance encouraged me to record my experiences. Special thanks also to my sisters, Dolores Rezendes and Maureen Stano, and my brother, Steve O'Reilly, who are always there when needed and who will never stop looking out for their kid sister.

My physician Henry M. Frey, M.D., who has steadfastly cared for my physical, emotional, and spiritual well-being since 1987. He is my role model for human compassion and service to others.

My mentor and friend Steven Schnur who, with his wife, Nancie, persuaded me to keep writing. His incisive comments truly helped shape this book.

My adviser and close friend Father Robert Warren, S.A.,

who stressed the importance of going public and giving a human face to AIDS.

My agent, Jillian Manus, who had the faith to take on an unproven writer and a controversial subject. My editor, Susan Suffes, who respectfully preserved the integrity of my experiences. And my early advocate, Liza Dawson, whose interest in this work set in motion the series of events that culminated in its publication.

My fellow activists and colleagues serving the HIV-affected population, whose selfless commitment strengthened my own resolve to help.

And all of the people I've known who have struggled against HIV/AIDS. Their ability to live fully in the face of their own suffering inspired the very heart of *Sarah's Song*.

Contents

SARAH'S SONG

Author's Note

Sarah's Song is autobiographical; its characters derive from actual individuals. Wherever possible I have maintained original names. However, some names have been changed in deference to the wishes of those involved or my inability to confirm their preference.

This book follows a journal format, and its structure therefore depends on time-anchored pieces written as the events described unfolded. While I felt it important to preserve their contemporary nature, I also felt it important to sometimes interject my present voice, with all its retrospective benefits. These insertions are generally italicized or otherwise set apart from the main text.

Foreword

This journal went in and out of drawers for years, incessantly nagging at me to keep writing even when I didn't feel much like reliving my experiences on paper. As I wrote, I began to sense that perhaps this story was not ultimately mine to keep. That feeling intensified when my husband, Bill, and I went public with our disease and realized that telling our story could change lives, even save lives. So I kept my journal current and enrolled in a writing class in 1993 to see if others thought my entries had any literary merit. The response was overwhelmingly positive. Conceived in 1987, *Sarah's Song* in its present form was finally born almost eight years later.

I encountered a number of obstacles during the process of writing *Sarah's Song*. Illness, unpredictable and debilitating, often prevented me from writing. Then there was the very character of the work, which required me not only to expose my own life and soul to public scrutiny, but my husband's as well. Prior to publication, I experienced many anxiety-filled moments when I questioned my portrayal of Bill's story, and my very right to do so. Fortunately, I am comforted by the memory of his support of this book—in fact, his insistence that I write it—and his full knowledge and approval of what it contained.

But I think the most difficult part of writing this book was not knowing how or when it would end, and fearing that the end would be written for me in effect by one or more capricious opportunistic infections. Like many people, I prefer a story that has a clear beginning, middle, and end. I realize now that my drawer-stuffings resulted from the fear that what I perceived to be the beginning and the middle of my book might in fact turn out to be its end.

I wrongly believed that *Sarah's Song* had to close with my death. Since I couldn't describe this event, I found myself unable to move ahead. There was also a part of me that felt that completing this book would give me permission to die.

As you might imagine, I have suffered some serious episodes of writer's block.

Once I realized that dying from AIDS pales in comparison to living with AIDS, I was able to move ahead and finish *Sarah's Song*. I am grateful that I maintained the health and determination necessary to write its final words myself.

Instead of giving me permission to die, the book's completion has given me a renewed desire to live. The process of writing it showed me that limits can and should be pushed and that we should not always assume we know what constitutes the beginning, middle, or end of any life.

Janice A. Burns

To you I will give the song of the sea,
The whisper of an elm, the laugh of a brook.
You will rest in the arms of a fragrant tree
And on its leaves you will write the pages of your book.
To you I will give a castle of gold
With windows of diamonds and doorknobs of pearls
And in its fine turrets the wind you will hold
While the teasing breeze tousles your buttercup curls.
To you I will give a steady hand to hold,
A shoulder to sleep on, two lips to kiss.
I will surrender my warmth to keep you from cold
And not one special moment of your life will I miss.
Ah, yes, how unreal my innocent hope seems.
If I could give but one thing, I'd give you my dreams.

"Sarah's Song," December 15, 1980

This is the first page of a book whose end I hope will come in thirty or forty years, and not in 1988 or 1989.

I am a white, married twenty-four-year-old woman who lives in Yonkers, New York. My husband and I earn $67,000 a year and spend most of it on vacations and home furnishings. We love to eat out, go to Broadway shows, and shock people by revealing the liberal outlooks that hide under our conservative exteriors. We call each other "booby" and call on our doctor every four weeks. We spend $1,200 a month on prescription drugs, and we will never have children. In October we will celebrate our third wedding anniversary; we have known each other for five years.

We are HIV-positive.

We are just two of the millions of "body positives" who unknowingly move in and out of your life every day, and this is probably just one of thousands of books-in-perpetual-progress being written by others like me. I'm not yet privy to its ultimate message or to the ultimate outcome of the events I describe. I do not know if this book will span twenty or two thousand pages.

I do know, however, that I must relate the very strange experience that is AIDS.

Because of legal, social, and moral implications, I have not yet told anyone about our situation save our doctor, his secretary, and our dentist. I may have unknowingly informed scores of Blue Cross employees via scores of insurance submissions. They in turn may have told my personnel representative, the president of the university in which I work, and my boss.

I have not yet told my mother or my father. . . .

PART ONE: 1987

I never thought my life would be such a quick read,
a condensed book.

Reeling In the First Months

There is no clever way to begin. The only way to start is to say that my husband has tested positive for the virus that causes AIDS, and he may die. And in six days I must take the same test.

I am twenty-three. He is twenty-two.

I knew of Bill's past, but it wasn't until I read an article in *US News and World Report* that we both sensed danger, an insistent pull at the corners of awareness, a long-forgotten ache suddenly rediscovered. Even when Bill went for his test three weeks ago, it seemed a formality, a necessary albeit stressful reassurance that our lives would remain unchanged. And the night before the results came back, we joked about how we would catch up on three weeks of self-imposed abstinence.

However, an innocuous reaction, a few antibodies in a test tube ensure that our periods of abstinence will become more prolonged, our moments of indulgence carefully sheathed and restrained.

I am twenty-three. He is twenty-two.

The current test, the one Bill took and I will take, is inhumane. It promises fetid swamps and blinding mists but offers no terrain-savvy guide, or even a lantern. It merely shows that you have been exposed to HIV. It doesn't reveal whether you presently have or will eventually develop full-scale disease. But suddenly I must contemplate the likelihood that my husband will sicken and die more quickly than other twenty-two-year-old husbands. And while I know I should dwell on positive things, like the fact that he is healthy and strong, I have a new sense of impermanence, of slipping on an ice patch hidden beneath the snow. It would be better to know immediately if the disease is coming or if it will remain dormant forever.

Perhaps it would be better to know if disease is coming.

Perhaps it would be better not to know.

I feel selfish right now. I don't want to be left alone. I don't want Bill to suffer. I don't want to forgo the experience of childbirth.

But I may be left alone.

I will witness Bill's suffering.

I will probably never have a child.

These thoughts make my throat throb and choke as if I had swallowed a hard-edged mint.

I really don't believe that Bill or I will die from AIDS. Is this merely a psychological defense, or is it a deep subconscious knowledge? I keep hoping that the test results were misread, but I know this hope is hysterical, irrational.

Last night Bill noted how ironic it was that the state didn't require a blood test before it issued us a marriage license.

But had we known, had we been tested before marriage, what then? Would the very knowledge of infection have magically, instantly nullified years of saying "I love you," years of thinking of myself as half of a greater whole? Or would I have discarded Bill like a candy wrapper, thinking that he and his future suffering could just blow away with the wind?

The fact is this: I would have married Bill anyway, even if I had known he was HIV-positive.

(This sounds suicidal; who would willingly choose a path preordained for disaster? But Bill made me feel so complete that the thought of living without him frightened me more than the potential consequences of living with him.)

Here is another selfish thought: I am terrified of dying. Suddenly all my health problems from the past year seem more ominous than the simple rashes and common colds to which they were attributed. When I was sixteen and a melodramatic adolescent, I convinced myself I would die a premature death, a death before thirty, and be transformed into a glamorous, suffering heroine like the ones I had admired in novels.

I don't want tragedy or glamour now.

I simply want to live.

I don't want to treat Bill differently, baby him, mother him, smother him. I don't want to tiptoe around his feelings or never be angry or irritated with him again. I don't want to create feelings and passions between us that didn't exist before. I don't want to create an easily torn paper doll dependent on me for positioning, features flat and lifeless. I don't want us to have AIDS.

Bill was supposed to find an infectious-disease doctor today and make an appointment for a physical. I hope he did.

I hope he didn't.

February 10, 1987 _____

A week has passed, and I somehow still do all the same things: I go to work, do the laundry, hide my purse on the subway. This is shock, the means by which routines are maintained, facades reinforced in the presence of terror. At least during the day. Unfortunately, shock doesn't prevent me from crying in bed every night after Bill falls asleep, or from staring at his closed eyes and wondering if I will see his death approach. But until we know his health status, and until I have the HIV test, the reality of AIDS in my life remains that dull obstruction, that brittle candy unable to be comfortably swallowed.

Bill has an appointment next Wednesday with Dr. Henry Frey, an infectious disease specialist. I had an appointment yesterday for my test, but it was snowing and the roads were icy, so I rescheduled. I think the snow was too easy an excuse.

I think perhaps I am terrified.

February 23, 1987 _____

When I arrived at the Health Department today, I learned that the HIV test counselor wouldn't be in—my second cancellation. On the way home I pondered the elusive, even supernatural meanings behind this development: I'm meant to have a few more weeks of uninhibited living; I don't need to be tested, as Bill's results were obviously incorrect; I will now have time to discover the reason for this experience. And so on. In the midst of these existential conjectures, I called Dr. Frey's secretary, explained the situation, and will be tested by the doctor himself on Wednesday evening.

So much for hidden meanings.

Bill had a six o'clock appointment with the doctor; he

didn't get home until after nine. He described Dr. Frey as somewhat pompous, with a tendency to lecture. But he thinks Dr. Frey is smart, and will trust him with his life.

Now for the dreaded diagnosis: Bill is in excellent health, with no signs of AIDS-related complex, or ARC. This is the good news. The bad news is that Dr. Frey believes every HIV-positive person will eventually develop AIDS. The disease, he says, progresses relentlessly over a six- to seven-year period.

Bill is currently classified as HIV-positive but asymptomatic. The doctor thinks he will prove an interesting case; Bill is the healthiest infected person he's seen thus far.

What price glory?

To date, Dr. Frey has treated twenty-five heterosexual couples. In all of these cases the man is infected; in only seven cases, however, has the virus spread to the female partner. I can only pray we don't bring this number to eight.

On Dr. Frey's advice, Bill applied for another life insurance policy.

Jesus, he's only twenty-two.

I learned yesterday that a close acquaintance is pregnant and expecting a baby in the fall. How can sex be so life-producing in one case and so life-destroying in another?

(I didn't know how to react to the news of this pregnancy. Whether to pity the expectant mother because she was young and alone. Whether to be happy because she would bring a new life into the world. Whether to despise her because she would experience what I already sensed I would never experience. What I should have felt is still subject to some debate. What I actually felt was this: I should be having that baby.)

February 26, 1987   _____

Dr. Frey drew my blood last night. His office is in an isolated dark lot, a place suggestive of squalor and back-alley
abortions. *(What I could not, or would not, see that night was
that I had traveled to a nice office park in a good part of the
city. Bill and I later bought a condominium in the same
neighborhood.)* I was shocked that all of the patients in the
waiting room were women. They all were terrified.

Or so they appeared to me.

When Dr. Frey entered the examining room, he flipped off
the wall switch and shone a light in my eyes; he believes
overall health is reflected here. He took one test tube of my
blood, and we proceeded to talk about AIDS.

Our conversation eventually turned to pregnancy and the
transmission of HIV from mother to child. Despite his
Catholicism, Dr. Frey feels that an HIV-positive woman
should probably abort if she becomes pregnant. He said he
couldn't, in good conscience, recommend that I carry a
baby if I test HIV-positive; it would be too dangerous. And
any child born to me would also suffer, regardless of her
own HIV status. Any child born to me would have to be
repeatedly stuck with needles during her first two years to
determine if HIV transmission occurred. An uninfected
child, while spared the physical consequences of my disease, would nonetheless suffer the premature loss of her
mother. And an HIV-infected child would not be spared
anything; she would shrivel up, burn with pain, die tragi-
cally young.

These harsh words were designed to shield me from a pre-
ventable source of future suffering, were designed to show
me that childlessness was not the worst thing that could happen to me.

I agree with his logic and trust his experience treating

HIV-infected babies. But would I really be so rational if I learned I was both pregnant and positive?

Wouldn't I want to leave behind some tangible evidence of the love Bill and I share, wouldn't I want to leave behind evidence of our very existence? Wouldn't I want to hide behind the veneer of a normal twenty-something married woman thrilled with her first pregnancy, and carry to term despite the danger to myself and my child?

As it is, I'm already overdue for my period this month.

March 16, 1987 _____

Whether from stress or from desperate desire, I never did get my period. And, true to my rather oversensitive nature, I exhibited all the early signs of pregnancy, transforming a headache here or nausea there into a harbinger of future delivery. This pregnancy would be okay; it had gotten in under the wire; it happened before I knew I shouldn't let it happen. I went to a walk-in clinic and was pricked again while chatting happily about pregnancy. Several days later the technician called me at work; she sounded heartbroken.

"I'm really sorry," she said.

I felt true hate for the first time in my life, hate toward chemicals in test tubes. In my case, the wrong test was positive; the right one, negative.

I am relieved and devastated. The relief comes from being spared a painful decision. If I were pregnant, I would probably have an abortion anyway, since I could test HIV-positive any time during the next six months. But I am devastated because I considered this our last chance to have a baby.

What a pessimistic view to take when a cure could be discovered any day.

Last week Bill received the results of his second test. All the crazy hopes I harbored about the corruption of the first one shattered when Dr. Frey confirmed the original diagnosis. He did say that Bill's other blood values look good and that he will probably remain healthy for the next few years.

I think I'm supposed to be happy.

March 19, 1987   _____

My test came back positive. I've been exposed to HIV, and there's a good chance I'll die far too young. I don't know what to feel, to do, to think, to expect, to care about. This is not glamorous, exciting, or dramatic; this is terror unadulterated.

When Dr. Frey told me, I was calm and controlled. And I remained so when I, in turn, told Bill.

"Well," I said, icy, brittle. "I have it too."

Bill called me at work later that day to comfort me, to commiserate, but I could hardly speak. I apologized for my earlier coldness, but even my apology lacked warmth. I don't want to resent him or blame him. I don't want these feelings, but part of me is so angry, has been so angry since he tested positive, that I dream of slapping and punching and inflicting pain. I went to Mass on my lunch hour and took Communion, but my prayer was not for acceptance.

It was simply: "Help me. Cure me."

I should be writing lofty treatises about a life hereafter, about appreciating each day. But I want *this* life, not another life in an unknown dimension. I want to grow old with Bill and have his babies, write a great novel, be a great musician. I want a house with so much land that neighbors won't breathe down our necks. I want to garden, take photographs, sew, create.

I don't want to die yet.

The doctor told me to try to live a normal life for now.

I have already forgotten what a normal life is.

The First Notes of the Song

July 11, 1984

I realized tonight how easy it is to imagine spending my life with Bill. I've never felt this way before, despite words I've used in the past to convince myself otherwise. There is no catch in the back of my mind, no uncertainty when the future and Bill are intertwined. I remember saying to him once in London that I needed him as I'd never needed anyone before. If he were here with me tonight, I would tell him the same, except I'd add: "and I'll never need anyone as much as I need you now, as much as I'll need you forever."

Three elderly nuns met our limousine as it pulled up in front of my high school alma mater. They whisked me through old wooden passages to the chapel, hiding me in deference to superstition or some vague law of God. I heard the organist play Bach, and I looked into the holy water font and thought, I am going to get sick right this minute.

I didn't, of course, and my parents gently walked me down the aisle, one on either arm. Out of the corner of my eye I saw the balcony filled to capacity with Ursuline nuns, perched and clucking kindly like pigeons in a coop. My father excused himself when we reached the altar; as a

Catholic deacon, he would perform the marriage ceremony, and he had to cover his tux with sacred vestments.

I've seen a snapshot of Bill taken that day. In it, he stands beside his best man, and he is pale. Pale as a pair of brand-new sneakers, pale as a glass of milk, pale as infection rendered him in later years. It was October 12, 1985, barely six months after our college graduation. We were young: Bill was still a month shy of his twenty-first birthday, and I had just turned twenty-two.

I first met Bill in June 1983 at a student research conference at Oberlin College. I attended the orientation session with about thirty other students; we eyed each other nervously while drinking Rolling Rock beer.

A voice behind me said, "Hi. My name's Bill, and I'm the center for the Villanova Wildcats."

I turned and looked up, expecting to find a tall, gangling basketball player. Instead, I saw nothing. When I lowered my gaze to about an inch below eye level, however, I saw a gorgeous, smiling man in a purple Izod shirt. It was my first encounter with Bill's wonderful sense of humor. I thought: This man has the face of a movie star. I think I fell in love with him at that moment.

But we didn't become romantically involved until 1984. During the seven-month period between our first meeting and our first kiss, I stayed with an old boyfriend, and Bill embarked on the same-sex relationship we believe left us both HIV-positive. Bill had struggled with his sexual identity since high school, without resolution. Perhaps my apparent rejection of him prompted his actions during the summer of 1983; perhaps my rejection came at a time when Bill felt unsure of himself, particularly with regard to male-female relationships. Perhaps what happened would have happened despite me.

I will never know.

Bill's relationship lasted only a few months, then ended.

We talked about it while he lived it. We joked that we would have to sleep together even if he was gay, just to have a child. Somewhere along the line we decided we would make wonderful parents.

During this period Bill wrote in a letter to me, "Thank God there was a Plato so that we can have this Platonic relationship."

We went to England as student researchers in January 1984. We pooled our resources with a third student and rented a flat in Camden Town. From the moment we moved in, Bill and I lived as a couple. We worked hard; we researched; we wrote our reports. We cooked proper English meals and played snooker and drank pints at the Mornington Arms. We traveled to Paris, Rome, Dublin. We favored Sacre Coeur to Notre Dame, and lit a candle there together one warm Paris evening, each with a hand on the taper. We found out years later that we had both prayed to be together for the rest of our lives.

Our prayers were answered. Or so we thought.

Bill proposed to me during our senior year in college, in the traditional way: on his knees, voice shaking, ring in hand. I had traveled to Pennsylvania from my school in Washington, D.C., to be with him for his twentieth birthday. That weekend was joyous. We spent hours planning for what we thought would be a charmed future together.

About six weeks after Bill's twentieth birthday, I became very sick with a high fever and numbing fatigue. Repeated tests for mononucleosis were negative, yet I had to leave school early that semester because of illness. In retrospect, it seems likely that I was seroconverting. Which means I most likely contracted HIV during the weekend Bill asked me to marry him.

During our first year of marriage, we established our rhythm together. After honeymooning in New England during the peak of fall foliage, we settled into a rent-controlled three-room apartment in Yonkers, New York. We stripped the floors, painted the kitchen yellow, made our tiny walk-up as unapartmentlike as possible.

By all accounts, we were nauseatingly cute. We traveled extensively, ate in the best restaurants, had season tickets to the Met, had a nice car, nice stereo, nice credit card balances. Our life could hardly have been any better, and we had the same dreams as any other young professional couple. We assumed we would buy a house, in Washington or San Francisco or London. We investigated Ph.D. programs and looked into married student housing at Harvard. We planned to have children, never thinking we might not be able to have them. We glided along the surface of life, blithely assuming that success would be ours, that happiness would be ours, that the future would be ours for the taking.

Barely six months after the brides of Christ nodded and wiped their eyes at the beauty of our wedding, I began to get sick. The skin on my face popped orange blisters that drained, peeled, and blistered again. I went to general practitioners; I went to specialists. I had biopsies, I took steroids, I applied lotions, but nothing worked. One theory was that I had an environmental allergy to something in my office. The more popular theory, held by both doctors and family members, was that I was nervous and somehow self-inflicting these symptoms. The only commonality I could find between the two theories was my job, which I quit in desperation as my skin buckled. Not long afterward the condition finally cleared up, and I began to believe that perhaps I was mentally unstable.

But almost immediately on the heels of this minor recovery came another bout with illness: glands so swollen that my voice sounded as if I spoke with a clothespin attached to my nose. I went the round of doctors again, until surgery was scheduled. My tonsils and adenoids came out on New Year's Eve 1986; the surgeon later remarked they were the largest he'd ever encountered. But I don't remember him being overly concerned as to why a twenty-three-year-old woman suffered from this condition.

I began paying more attention to media stories about a disease that was killing young people. This was 1987, and the stories were about AIDS. But to Bill and me, AIDS was a disease that only attacked drug abusers, Haitians, and what we then considered to be highly promiscuous homosexuals, men who had sex with hundreds, even thousands of partners. The five partners we had accumulated between us hardly seemed significant.

Yet my health problems persisted. Compelled by some inner dread, I searched the newsstands for information on AIDS. I read everything I could find, and knew what had to be done. Bill bravely made an appointment for an HIV test, while I waited with my symptoms in hand, too frightened to be tested myself.

Bill was tested anonymously at a clinic in affluent Westchester County. In 1987 it took three weeks to obtain the results.

During those three weeks we convinced ourselves that we'd overreacted, that we had nothing to worry about. We thought we would be able to forget those weeks. We sincerely believed their impact would prove minimal.

Three weeks later Bill returned to the Health Department. I did not go with him; after all, his test was going to come back negative. It was not going to be a big deal.

During the late morning, my phone rang at work. It was Bill.

"Guess what," he said, voice lifeless. "My test came back positive."

It was a cold day in February. Bill called me from a pay phone on a street corner. He stood at that phone as the snow covered the ground and covered his hair. He then walked back to the car and cried, a lonely, shivering man who had *just received his death sentence. I don't know why he didn't jam the exhaust pipe right then, get it over with quickly.*

Perhaps he looked at the wedding ring on his left hand.

I arrived home before Bill that evening. I walked into the apartment and could do nothing but put my head down and cry. I raised it only when I heard Bill's key in the lock. We looked at each other wordlessly, he from the metal-framed doorway and I from my hard wooden chair. Then he came over and knelt in front of me, as if he were proposing all over again.

He knelt and he laid his head in my lap and we remained entwined for a long time, swaying slightly to the music of sorrow.

Sarah

Can ovaries scream?

I think mine did when I heard the wails of the newborn down the hall. I doubled over as if punched, eyes blurry, knees gelatinous. I hungered to break down the door, comfort the baby, interrogate the parents, demand they never consider this child a nuisance, never wish that its attachment could have been intercepted by drugs or a vacuum pump. I wanted to take that baby away from its mother, cover it with my body, die for it if necessary.

My ovaries are probably shriveled and mangled by now, eaten through with foreign chemicals and mutating cells. And if they still live, they could be lethal. They could produce a 1980s thalidomide baby, arms stubby and body stunted from the AZT* I'm certain I will eventually take. Or,

*These were my early fears, when the effects of AZT were still largely unknown. I now know these fears were unfounded; today pregnant women are routinely advised to take AZT to reduce the risk of HIV transmission from mother to child. There has, in fact, been no epidemic of "AZT babies."

worse yet, they could hatch a sweet and beautiful child who would die slowly and miserably, loving her mother to the end, despite the fact it was her mother's selfishness that made her live and made her die.

Bill is superb with children, and they are invariably drawn to him. I began to love children myself after meeting Bill; I watched him and understood kindness in its purest form. We decided early to have a child together. We thought as well that this would be one lucky child. So we married and assumed that raising babies would be as routine as brushing our hair or reading the morning papers.

But then the doctor said, "You, too."

When I was a freshman in college, my boyfriend's contraceptive failed—that is, the condom broke. I missed my period, and my roommate and I went to a Maryland clinic filled with young couples and solitary women. I had decided: if pregnant, I would abort. I planned to hock my television and typewriter and borrow the rest of the necessary fees. The tired counselor told me to come back when I was two weeks overdue. I returned to my room shaken, unable to nerve myself for another trip to that barren office in Bethesda. I got my period two days later.

To this day, I feel as if I'd actually had that abortion. The commitment to the act was formulated, firm, its eventual outcome reduced to a mere financial matter.

I dreamed for years about my unconceived and unaborted child; I named her Sarah. I dreamed she was a brown earthworm I held gently in my mouth, who trusted me to protect her. Instead I swallowed her whole like a chewed piece of gum.

To me, she lived and died.

I would do anything to have Sarah back.

Lapses

I went to see Dr. Frey last week, and mercifully, I learned that I'm in excellent health. We talked for a long time; I've never been to a doctor who *talks* so much with his patients. I learned a lot more about the virus, and even received "homework"—to read articles about HIV's close relative, the visna virus in sheep.

At one point during the evening, Dr. Frey said, "You're too healthy. Don't let me hurt you."

I think he meant: "Don't let me use you to experiment with AZT." But he didn't actually say these words, and I didn't actually ask him what he meant. I find myself doing this a lot lately, not asking questions when perhaps I should. Sometimes I don't feel like hearing the answers.

Although generally an upbeat visit, there was one disturbing moment. Dr. Frey asked, "How's your memory?"

My memory is fine, but Bill's memory has been shaky for

a while. Recently, for example, we were on our way to visit friends in New Jersey. Bill apparently forgot where we were headed and started driving in the wrong direction. He also frequently forgets his reason for entering a room, or forgets what year he graduated from high school.

I have to wonder whether these are normal slips, inconsequential reactions to too many new and disturbing facts, or whether they are symptomatic of something larger. I've read that memory loss is one of the first signs of AIDS itself, manifested as a kind of early senility. We try to maintain a positive attitude, but we're frightened.

Bill is with Dr. Frey as I write. I dread his diagnosis.

I don't want Bill to die.

June 9, 1987 _____

As I feared, Dr. Frey was concerned about Bill's memory problems. He took a lot of blood and scheduled Bill for a CAT scan of the head. This, paired with a spinal tap, should reveal any central nervous system damage. Bill has to decide whether or not to agree to the spinal tap, although I think he will do whatever is necessary to survive, no matter how unpleasant.

If there is central nervous system involvement, Bill will take AZT. How long does he have after that point? Is neurological damage the first labored step on the road to death?

I can't even contemplate that possibility yet.

Bill's CAT scan is scheduled for ten-thirty this morning. He took the day off from work, pleading allergy tests. I wonder if he will run out of plausible excuses for his absences, and if he should hoard these excuses for future use, like he would pennies in an empty wine bottle?

Marking Eternity

Here is a warm memory that burrows deeply under the covers on a snowy morning, as comforting as fuzzy socks and strong tea with lots of honey:

My father stands in front of an easel in the spare bedroom we called the "painting room," a photograph of a pretty, peaceful scene—an Arizona sunset or a cow ambling down a country road—clipped to the corner of the canvas. Johnny Mathis sings "Chances Are" in a duet with my father, who squeezes the notes out of one side of his mouth while blowing cigarette smoke out of the other. The upright piano stands against one wall, and our brand-new stereo with its state-of-the-art record-stacker sits on the triangular corner desk my father recently antiqued in forest green. He holds a beer in his left hand and wears threadbare paint-speckled jeans. I am a shy child, and although it is a clear summer day, I prefer to be indoors with my father instead of outdoors with friends. He shows me for the hundredth time how to mix paints on the palette, but even today I have no flair for working in color. However, like him, I stack up the records during the act of creation.

Why do I so vividly remember this scene today? Why do so many long-forgotten memories resurge lately?

The reason may be as simple as this: I can picture myself in scenes from the past—the way I looked, what I said, how I felt. These scenes are incorruptible; I am incorruptible. When I try to think of myself in a future place—say, five years from now—I cannot. Is it any wonder that I prefer my safe memories, my days when my father painted beautiful, impossible landscapes unsullied by human hands?

Although I constantly tell myself that being HIV-positive is not the same as being dead, I nonetheless feel pressured to make my mark in eternity before I become too sick or too incoherent to try. But it is this compulsion, not this virus, that stops me dead in my tracks. To act is possibly to err. And with a limited supply of actions left to me, I cannot afford to make any mistakes.

So I do not act, do not do the things I always said I would do if I knew my days were numbered. I do not write consistently; I do not reconcile broken friendships. I do not show my vulnerability, or utter loving, kind words. Inactivity is my weapon against the dangers in my life, the things I most fear.

How do others rise above the specter of their own death, elude their own ghosts in the whispers of early morning, in the shouts of everyday life?

Especially when they've just turned twenty-four?

Lobsters

"Nuzzle my nozzle," Bill says during one of our increasingly infrequent moments of intimacy.

His attempted vulgarity, so inconsistent with his proper, refined demeanor, tickles me like a long feather. He smiles, too, although he tries hard to be seriously lecherous.

Sex was always something we didn't have to think about; we'd often collapse and sarcastically sigh: "It's a shame we're not compatible!" We used to make love often; now we rarely do. Here is logic: soon after learning I was HIV-positive, I went off the Pill and turned to the so-called barrier methods of protection. My rationalization: the Pill was too toxic for a diseased body. I cried during our first episode with a condom. I was so pleased we still worked, like flashlights that obligingly shine during a blackout.

I am selfish; I should go back on the Pill. I rebel; each dose reduces my limited supply of potential babies. I am in denial; I will recover and have a normal, healthy child—that is, if somehow AZT does not leave us sterile.

Soon after diagnosis, I became more Catholic in my practices: no sex except for the purpose of procreation; hence, no sex.

I punished Bill, I punished myself. Since his body got me into this, he could not have mine until he begged my forgiveness. He in turn punished me; in his mind, he had already done enough damage. AIDS made us reject the act underlying our disease. AIDS, in effect, made us reject the one act that could have provided a measure of comfort.

We still punish each other. Frigid at twenty-four; legs needing to be cracked open.

Lobsters.

I'd be lying if I said I never thought about AIDS in my life until I knew AIDS was in my life.

In my mind, AIDS existed like any other current event. If the facts interested me, I absorbed them. Otherwise, they swiftly entered and exited my mind. With its undercurrent of sinfulness, AIDS intrigued me when it seeped into my everyday life. But this didn't happen too often, and I held AIDS at arm's length and observed it only as a phenomenon worthy of my sociology degree. But it would be a lie to say I first heard the term "AIDS" on a winter's day in 1987.

I had heard it before.

I just never listened.

Why did AIDS take me so by surprise, a girl who grew up in a tough neighborhood, a girl who was relatively street-smart? Why did I think AIDS happened only to other people? It makes no sense in retrospect, but so often the truth doesn't make sense. Perhaps if I tell you my story, you will understand my relative nonchalance better than I do myself.

I grew up in the Bedford Park section of the Bronx, within walking distance of Fordham University and a short bus ride to the zoo. Racial and ethnic tensions permeated a neighborhood that was once the exclusive domain of the white middle class. Once, I remember watching from my bedroom window as a gang of teenage boys armed with bats and knives torched a car. I couldn't even tell if the boys were white or black or Hispanic. It didn't matter; this was what the gangs did in the seventies.

I knew every stairwell, every roof, every uneven surface of that neighborhood from hours of playing block tag and off-the-point. I also knew what and whom to avoid. I avoided the people who lived down the block because they stole from the stores and later burned down their building for the insurance money. I avoided the school yard. I avoided an apartment in my own building known to house drug dealers and prostitutes. I learned from an early age to carry my keys in my hand, point side out, like a switchblade. I learned to walk down the middle of the street and avoid the alleys and doorways where dangerous people lurked.

It was a neighborhood rough enough that I quit my high school job at a fast-food restaurant to avoid a pimp who patiently stood by my cash register and tried to sell me a new career. A neighborhood where drugs and alcoholism and abuse were prevalent enough to make me feel blessed to have the family I had.

My neighborhood may have been tough, but my own life was not. I attended Catholic school, I sang in the choir, I never did anything remotely illegal. My life was so safe that I found myself attracted to people and situations that were not—unusual people, creative people, brilliant people on the fringes of acceptability.

Perhaps I wanted to escape my own history and live more of the excitement around me. And part of my history found me in the role of minister's daughter. My father discovered late in life that he had a religious calling, and was ordained a deacon in 1978. Both of my parents thus became leaders in the local church, and with their new responsibilities came my own to be a model of propriety, of virtue, of grace. None of this was said to me, but it was so heavily woven through the fabric of my life that I wore the garments of conservatism and compliance as if they were my natural skin.

Until, of course, I hit adolescence, when I rebelled in the conventional ways.

With a phony ID, I snuck into bars at sixteen. I smoked cigarettes on school grounds at lunchtime. I dyed my hair green for punk rock parties. My rebellion was mild enough that I was able to maintain my grades and edit the yearbook and take piano lessons. A rebel at heart, I was hardly a rebel in fact.

I looked for the exciting part of me while I remained a nice kid who gave little trouble. I looked for ways to rebel while winning scholarships to college, winning awards for community service, winning, winning, winning, while writing poems about death and betrayal and hypocrisy, and winning awards for these, too.

At sixteen, I found my calling. I would be a writer and live the life of an artist. I would have affairs with my professors; I'd travel around the world with nothing but my typewriter and the clothes on my back. A good writer, I thought, has to live life in all its permutations, has to write from experience. At the time, "experience" meant the great realm of things I'd never tried—namely sex and drugs. I set out to grow up and shed my Catholic schoolgirl image. I remember sitting in the high school cafeteria after one of my first dates and thinking to myself: "I am a woman now."

Sex quickly lost its promise to transform my life. I reverted to my natural prudishness and dated harmless boys and fell in love every two weeks. I smoked marijuana a couple of times, and was unimpressed. I never had the nerve or desire *to try anything stronger, never once did the cocaine favored by some of my rich acquaintances. Despite my efforts, I was not the rebel I dreamed I was. I lived the fast life vicariously, content to watch other people's forays into the unknown. It was in high school that I adopted my tolerant attitude toward morality and choices. Novelty was my ticket to worldliness, and I embraced it philosophically, even if I did not embrace it literally.*

I attended Trinity College in Washington, D.C., on a presidential scholarship. It was there I found a way to differentiate myself, although not in a way I expected. Soon after I started college, a friend of mine was raped by a stranger who dragged her from a bus stop to a deserted school yard. I was the only person she told at first; I spent many hours listening to her relive the event, listening to her blame herself for its occurrence. I didn't know anything about rape, didn't know how to help someone in so much pain.

So I set out to learn everything I could about sexual violence—its legal, social, psychological consequences. I read Against Our Will *by Susan Brownmiller; I traveled to England in my junior year to research grass-roots responses to rape. I heard stories I never wanted to hear, stories about the brutality of brothers and fathers, of violence and victimization and virulent hatred.*

I was never the same person again. I had truly lost my innocence.

After returning from England, I continued to talk about topics normally kept in the closet, even at my women's college: date rape, domestic violence, women's rights. In a school where almost everyone ordered the same clothes from L. L. Bean and hoped to marry a Georgetown man, I was an anomaly. I hung out with a small group of girls who acted in ways offensive to the majority of students; we became known informally as "the iconoclasts." After years of trying to be different, I finally succeeded in being different without really trying.

I felt strangely validated when in my senior year I found the following graffiti scrawled on a bathroom wall on campus: "Kill the iconoclasts."

In a way, then, I was primed for the drama, the discomfort, the difference I would later experience so intensely; perhaps I should have expected them. Yet, in the early 1980s, when news of an epidemic in Haiti and news of a gay cancer reached my ears, I heard but didn't listen. When a few years later it became clear that a domino effect was in play, that sharing partners and sharing needles and sharing blood meant sharing risk, I heard but didn't listen. When Bill and I talked about our past lives spent out of each other's company, I was so in love with him already that I heard but believed our love would somehow protect us.

Early in my relationship with Bill, I saw a news segment about a couple who were not allowed to marry in Saint Patrick's Cathedral in New York because the groom had AIDS. I was outraged, and for the briefest moment—I remember this quite distinctly—I put myself in the bride's place. It certainly crossed my mind that Bill could be at risk for HIV, but he was such a careful person, so in control all the time, that AIDS was inconsistent with my idea of him. I think AIDS was inconsistent with his own idea of himself.

In addition, Bill was healthy, and I thought people with HIV died within six months of diagnosis; therefore, I thought, he must have escaped infection. I thought of AIDS only briefly when I thought of Bill. Thought briefly, in a self-congratulatory way, of nursing him during his final days, which I assumed would come when he was seventy or eighty years old. Thought briefly of AIDS and allowed my head to know that Bill represented a certain danger while my heart gladly accepted that danger. Accepted that danger especially when I heard his intimate hello over the phone or saw the way he looked at me in a crowd, a way that bade me drop everything and follow.

From its very beginning, our life together was not what we thought it was. AIDS was always with us; it was there during our first kiss in 1984. It was there when we stood before my father and spoke our wedding vows. It was there all the time, in the air around us, seen and fleetingly acknowledged and brushed away as casually as ants at a picnic.

We brushed it away because two people so much in love would have to be immune from the ravages of AIDS.

Wouldn't they?

PART TWO: 1988

What made me think that the terminally ill possess a greater understanding of life? Why did I think they were magically transformed into martyrs, saints?

I hardly feel like a saint or martyr.

I feel more like a sacrificial lamb desperately trying to avoid the knife that will slit my throat.

Mirror Images

It is a weekday morning, a morning when spring kisses the air like a lover, and I lie sluggishly on my Haitian cotton sofa, a thermometer, a medical encyclopedia, and a bathwater-spotted copy of *Jane Eyre* my only companions. I will play hooky from my university job today. Lingering bone aches and light-headedness, plus the thought of dealing with lifeless piles of paper, make pulling on stockings and putting on makeup impossible chores. Yesterday I walked into work at eight-thirty and left at nine; today I didn't even stir when the alarm sounded. I feel infinitely more alive today, prone and passive, than I do on days spent soothing bosses and writing endless memos.

Sometimes I think I am well prepared for life as an invalid. Some people find comfort in chocolate or shopping or sex; my favorite pastime has always been to lie propped and rumpled on the living room couch surrounded by tissues and mugs of soothing drinks, reading, dozing, losing hours in an eye-blink. I always preferred plumped pillows to bosom buddies. As a child, I built a private fortress between the double doors of the hallway closet and stocked it with bed-spreads, books, and bottles. My repeated hospitalizations with asthma often landed me in a plastic oxygen tent, which was quickly strewn with titles like *Timmy Learns to Read* and *Alphabet Soup*. Despite the IV tubes inserted in my feet, I don't remember feeling particularly unhappy. I craved then, as I crave now, silence and solitude and literary escape.

For several days I have had a persistent low-grade fever. The medical encyclopedia I scrupulously explore suggests ovulation, influenza, bone cancer. The alert and active fragment of my brain urges me to get off the couch and call Henry* with my symptoms. The languorous librarian, however, won't surrender her cushions in order to grab the kitchen phone. So instead I stretch, resolve to be well by Monday, and indulge what I consider to be my naturally delicate constitution. Bill offers to drive me to the doctor's office. "Let's not overreact," I say.

I smile and pour myself a fourth cup of coffee, and just for a moment feel as snug as Jane felt in her window seat as I read her words: "What a consternation of soul was mine that dreary afternoon! How all my brain was in tumult, and all my heart in insurrection! Yet in what darkness, what dense ignorance was the mental battle fought! I could not answer the ceaseless inward question—*why* I thus suffered; now, at the distance of—I will not say how many years, I see it clearly."

Because I was a sickly child, I learned to find comfort in

---

*Dr. Henry Frey. In 1988 I started referring to him simply as Henry when I wrote, although I still addressed him more formally in person.

settings imposed by illness. After outgrowing my asthma, I still sought comfort the same way. Quietly. Keeping my mind off the problem at hand by reading. Setting up my world within easy reach in order to remain as independent as possible. It is how I still find comfort when the world becomes too painful; I reduce it to the realm of my couch, and wait for the pain to desist.

This long-practiced instinct to hibernate has rendered me decidedly unambitious. I have modest goals, at best. First and foremost, I want to get out of the city, which makes my glands throb and speckles my skin with dirt by day's end. I dream of a small, humble home (I admit it: a log cabin) with a stream at the property's edge; I will walk through the trees and understand God. The house empowers me to study, write, soothe troubled souls. Bill and I communicate wordlessly here; we make love on the rough stone floors and sprout child after child from the black dirt and running water.

These are my dreams: hushed and controlled, beautiful and reassuring. Currently, however, we have a one-bedroom in the city. We cram fashionable appliances into this space—tabletop grill, hand-held vacuum, electric anti-plaque toothbrush. Our plants are silk in lifelike soil. We spend much of our time planning, organizing, dreaming about that future day when everything will return to normal and we can get on with our lives for real.

But these plans must remain unrealized for now, perhaps forever; my gentle stream has a strong and perilous undercurrent. My long-practiced mornings on the couch, once soothing, are newly touched by panic. It is one thing to laze because you need a rest from the excesses of everyday normal life. It is quite another to take to bed because being ill is no longer a pretense.

Which is it this morning? A bit of both? More of one?

If invalidism causes me to take to my bed, then taking to

my bed will no longer be my preferred method of escape. I must find another outlet: a pad and pencil perhaps, or a screen covered with words.

Rethinking

_____

I went to see Henry last night to find out what to do for conjunctivitis and found out instead that I am his "star." My blood counts have stabilized, and, apart from this minor eye infection, my health is excellent. My clinical dips and blips will be immortalized on slides and presented at infectious-disease rounds held monthly at a major teaching hospital.

I also learned, however, that I was originally misdiagnosed as being asymptomatic. Henry now believes I already suffered from the progressive generalized lymphadenopathy (PGL) associated with AIDS-related complex when we first met. PGL is a fancy term for swollen glands run amok. My glands, particularly those in my neck, have been swollen for years, and it was this condition that first prompted me to search for the cause that eventually proved to be HIV. When one of the doctors in my increasingly long line of doctors removed my tonsils and adenoids, I don't think it ever crossed his mind that I might be HIV-infected; he probably never expected to find HIV in a middle-class married woman. I entered a new year eating ice cream in a hospital room, only two months from learning that hospital rooms and invasive treatments would probably be implicated in the start of every future year.

So I now must reconcile two thoughts: the belief that I was well and taking AZT only as prophylaxis, and the truth. That I wasn't well at all and AZT is actually a first-line treatment.

Apparently Bill is a star, too, in his own way. But I don't ask too many questions about his health, because I am afraid of what the answers might be. Bill is less stable than I am; some of his blood values are more affected than mine. He's had pinkeye for a month. He works too hard, sleeps too little, and doesn't show any emotion about his disease.

I want us to be the *National Enquirer*'s Miracle Couple: "The First to Be Cured of AIDS (and More in Love Than Ever!)"

I don't want one of us to live and one of us to die, but if it has to be this way, then I gladly give my star to Bill.

Contemplating Craziness

I idle in the parking lot and wait for Bill to arrive on the nine-thirty express. John Cougar rocks on my car radio; it is a perfect summer night.

Then it hits me: what if I go crazy before I die? This is a new thought, worse than any prospect of physical demise. My carefully nurtured social proprieties will dissolve: I will babble like a panhandler in Grand Central Station, strung out, uncomprehending, scratching all the wrong places in public.

Worse yet, if the dementia hits Bill. His exceptional intelligence, his analytical mind unable to assess big from small, shoe from glove, life from death. Would I kill him if he became demented, could I hold a pillow over his head before anyone else noticed the cognitive slips? Should I?

We must discuss this; after all, I should be certain that he would want to be smothered, that he wouldn't *want* to be alive and crazy. It is too gruesome to contemplate; perhaps we'll unhinge at precisely the same time and never realize each other's weakness. I take comfort in thinking that perhaps insane people mysteriously understand each other, that perhaps problems arise only when the crazy and the normal mix.

I once studied a particular polar bear at the Bronx Zoo. He was beautiful and strong, a majestic specimen, and I was repeatedly drawn to him throughout the day. Because, hour after hour, he did nothing but take five steps forward, then take five steps back: a kind of polar bear cha-cha-cha. Although most people laughed at him, I was distressed. Such a beautiful animal, but what a waste of energy, how useless his life had become. Did he realize that people ridiculed him, parodied his movements? Did he know how inappropriate his behavior was, and just not care? Or did he know and care about his inappropriateness, but couldn't do anything to stop it?

And which of these three possibilities is the most merciful?

If I become similarly deranged, if I become a dancing polar bear, will people laugh and point at me, saying, "What a tragedy, so beautiful, but what an imbecile!" This is uncharitable; human nature is not so cruel. Most people would look upon the lunatic me with pity and offer assistance. I am, after all, a human being and not a bear.

But if this happens, if I lose my mind from AIDS dementia; if I must lose my mind, then I would choose to lose it but never know it to be lost. And I would prefer the loss happen quickly, not slowly, not in the form of forgetting the president's name or forgetting to use a sanitary pad and being publicly humiliated.

No, I would prefer that it happen quickly, like a lightning bolt to the brain: strike, sizzle, silence. I witness Bill's memory lapses, his forgetting why he entered a room, or his forgetting where he should drive, and I wonder if I worry needlessly, or if these lapses are just a part of aging.

He is, after all, twenty-three.

Sometimes I think we are already mad from this disease. We do a regular one-two during our office visits. We joke; we act vibrant, sexual; we show great maturity toward our situation. I inevitably blow it, however, after the exam is over and we sit in Henry's office. My charm and energy dissipate, unfizz. Bill and Henry look at each other, knowing I fruitlessly await the magic words: "It's a miracle! You are the first person in the history of this disease to be cured!"

The rest of the fantasy is predictable: Bill will also be cured. We will take a deep breath and say "Phew! That was close!" and go on to have child after child conceived on the stone floor of a country house.

Or is this very fantasy the first sign of craziness?

Lies

A guy walks into a drugstore and asks the gay pharmacist if he has Ayds.

"God, I hope not!" he replies.

My disease used to be a diet pill, but I think the manufacturer changed its name.

My disease has been used as proof by the misinformed that justice truly exists. After all, its first victims were those destined for an early demise anyway. Hemophiliacs, who would be eradicated by a preexisting weakness in their bodies. Drug abusers and homosexuals, whose bodily weaknesses would be eradicated for them by the hand of the Lord. AIDS is perceived to jump from person to person as a bee jumps from flower to flower. Just the other day a friend of mine refused to go to a bachelorette party because she feared catching HIV from the male strippers who would be there. She is a nurse.

I knew she was wrong, but I chose not to correct her. I feared my words would inadvertently reveal the real reason for my dissension.

I think about disclosure every day. I weigh the fantasy options: Thanksgiving spent in a local diner versus eating too much Boston cream pie with my sisters. Doing girl-things with friends versus watching other people's lives on television. For eighteen months Bill and I have buried the fact of our infection under the familiar wrappings of a normal working couple. If we don't talk about it, it is not there. We don't tell anyone because we believe it's unkind to burden them unnecessarily. Especially when it's so obvious that a cure will come and save us any day now. A deus ex machina.

I fear disclosure for any number of reasons, all which involve rejection, and some which take precedence over others on any given day. Today my greatest fear is banishment from our godchild, the child born so soon after I learned I had HIV, so soon after I had been rendered sterile, for all practical purposes. The child given to our spiritual keeping in the Catholic tradition. The child who I felt was the nearest thing to Sarah I would ever get. On the day of her christening I held her while I stood on the altar with Bill; for that brief moment when the priest crossed her forehead with chrism, she was ours.

Later at the party I excused myself and cried huge gulping sobs, like a baby wailing for its mother's breast, and wept out once and for all the temptation to fertilize the ova my body still so meanly produced. I gave up the dream of my own child that day, and now I face the prospect that only a few simple words could cause me to lose another. Tonight it is too great a risk to take.

Day in and day out I think about disclosure. I feel I should come clean with my boss, a doctor. I think he must know or suspect something is wrong, but I've thought this before and have always been surprised that nobody suspects a thing. If I asked for advice on this matter, I know what I'd hear: don't tell your boss; you'll be fired or eased out or have your duties plucked away one by one until you are nothing more than a terminally ill liability sitting behind a desk, waiting for the day you can collect an entitlement.

However, how much longer can I lie? I've already used every imaginable excuse for missing work—sprained ankle, stomach flu, gynecological problems—each delivered in decreasingly convincing fashion. I spend thirty-five hours each week at work, ten hours commuting to work, and another ten thinking about work. My job absorbs the majority of my time each week. If this time is based on lies, I am becoming, or indeed have already become, a predominantly untruthful person. How much longer should I lie?

But today it is the fear of losing my godchild that keeps me quiet. More often, most often, it is the fear of losing my parents. My parents, for whom I was the different one, the one who wrote poetry, the one my mother felt so strongly about sending to college that she got an outside job to save money for tuition. The one who performed in a piano recital at a hotel down the block from Carnegie Hall, but whose parents thought it was as wonderful as if I had performed at the real thing. The one destined to escape the Bronx, who always publicly made them proud.

How will I possibly tell them that their prize, their pride, their daughter still introduced as "the baby," has AIDS?

And when do I schedule this revelation?

Between *Jeopardy!* and *Wheel of Fortune*?

My fears fertilize strong stalks of passivity; I am firmly planted in denial. My immunodeficiency syndrome is joined by another: the if-I-can't-see-it-it-must-not-exist complex.

Lies.

So we will do what we must do now, after zippering up for so long. We will tell only when it becomes imperative to tell, when the skin becomes loose on our bodies, when the sign on our hospital door carries a warning label like a pack of cigarettes. When the small cracks in the surface multiply with prolonged time and pressure until we finally shatter and the truth pours out, unadulterated, raw, bloody. When our carefully preserved jar of lies is full and its contents overflow.

I carry two distinct pictures of my father in my mind: the pre-God father of my early childhood, a man quick-tempered and a little wild, and the enlightened version who, in his forties, found himself pulled in directions he himself did not quite understand.

My father, like most fathers in my neighborhood, remained an enigma throughout my childhood. He worked as a typesetter in Manhattan and took the D train to and from work every day for most of his life. He provided for us steadily and abundantly, although he never spoiled us. From what I hear, he was a soft disciplinarian by the time I was born; already in his thirties, he had fathered the first of his three previous children when he was only seventeen. I think that by the time I came along, he was just tired.

My father was, and is, perpetually cheerful. He was in charge of waking us up for school, which he did by tickling our feet and mumbling "Time to get up!" through a mouthful of toothpaste. He is an inveterate pacer and can't stay still even if he is otherwise occupied. I also pace; I often find myself in the living room reading a book, half dressed, having wandered out of my bedroom while putting on my clothes. My father and I pace and ponder, but always somehow rediscover our original path.

My father expected his children to wake up as happy and alert as he did, and was merciless to this end. Many mornings I sat on my parents' bed and watched my father fold his handkerchief and fix his belt while he drilled me on current events.

"So what do you think about Watergate?" he'd ask at seven in the morning. I foggily struggled not only to be awake and pleasant but to remember everything connected to these unfathomable adult crises.

As my father entered middle age, he felt a pull toward the church. My parents were already very involved in our parish, and headed up various committees and clubs. One day my father asked God for a sign to illuminate his internal struggle, and stepped into a Midtown church on his way home from work. As he walked in, the priest was delivering his homily. From the altar he intoned: "You are called to serve."

It was the sign my father needed, and he entered the diaconate, which, in the Catholic church, is only one step below full priesthood. In this way, my father preserved his ties both to my mother and to God.

Daddy was a late bloomer. Ordained in his forties, he then proceeded to go to college for his bachelor's degree in psychology. He never stopped going to school, and several years later received his master's degree. Although not currently enrolled in classes, he plans to retire soon, and I suspect further education awaits.

Daddy bloomed late, but he bloomed well.

My father believes in miracles and signs, and fully trusts in things he cannot see. I have inherited this quality, al-

though sometimes I place too much emphasis on signs of life
and not enough emphasis on life itself. I have my father's red
hair and freckles, his wide feet and good teeth, his artistic
ability, and a sense of humor that all too often relies on well-
worn and thoroughly bad jokes: "People are dying to get in
there," he inevitably says when we pass a cemetery. We both
love music, and won a father-daughter dance contest held at
my high school when I was sixteen.

In many ways, we still dance to the same music.

My mother is quiet and reserved, a woman who I think
prefers the serenity and predictability of books and pets to
the chaos of people.

My mother unobtrusively imparted iotas of wisdom over
the years. One of the first bits of wisdom I remember is this:
"Don't call anyone stupid. A person may act in a stupid way,
but that doesn't make the person stupid."

Although I can think of a few people who might qualify as
exceptions, I generally think my mother is right. Intelligent
people sometimes act unwisely, but one unwise action should
not forever label a person. We always retain the ability to
improve upon our actions.

I don't remember ever calling anyone stupid in my life as
a consequence. Except, of course, my sister Dolores, who
caused me to break every self-imposed rule I had.

Another piece of my mother's wisdom was this: "Don't get
involved in things that could embarrass you."

This rule was a little harder to follow. Like any teenager—
or any adult, for that matter—I got myself into far too many
compromising situations and often found myself wishing I
had heeded my mother's advice in the first place.

And then there's the third truth: "Even the pope has to use
the bathroom." If my life depended on it, I couldn't tell you
what prompted this statement. Its message still rings loud
and clear, however: don't be impressed by appearances or

titles or possessions; no matter our station, we are all equally deserving humans in the end.

I am more like my mother than I sometimes care to admit, but this is hardly novel; it is the universal trait of mothers and daughters. Like my mother, I can hibernate for months, seeing few people, happily living in books until I realize that the sound of a single voice is a lonely sound indeed. Like my mother I often prefer to observe life from a safe distance. I think we are not aloof but shy, and we hide our shyness behind words and analyses and a sometimes sarcastic humor.

The trait I admired most growing up was my mother's unwavering loyalty to my father, both in public and in private. To the world, they presented a consolidated whole: respectful of each other, of similar opinions and interests, always each other's first priority. As a child, this bothered me; I wanted to be the center of my parents' universe. But my parents were, and are, each other's universe, and we children remain merely sources of light that shine upon their special world. Only as an adult can I appreciate the fact that, although loved, we were not chosen in the way my parents chose each other. They married at seventeen; forty-eight years later they are still together and, by all appearances, still in love.

My mother served as a female model of devotion and sacrifice. She is one of the few people who never once said or implied that I shouldn't care so much for Bill. Shouldn't, in fact, put my life on hold during those times when he needed all of my energy simply to live a life that quickly depleted his own. My mother unquestionably would do the same for my father, and therefore never questioned my sleepless nights, my days visiting him in hospitals, my moments of limiting my actions so Bill could keep up.

I never equated my mother's devotion with subservience or weakness. On the contrary, I find her devotion to be her greatest strength.

PART THREE: 1989

_____

The finest lesson my mother gave me was this:
If you choose to give yourself up to love,
then you'd better make sure your love is the greatest work
of your lifetime.

We Are Here But Cannot Speak

Bill and I recently saw a production of "AIDS Alive" by the People With AIDS Theater Group. It was short, only forty-five minutes long, and the actors' names in the photocopied program had been erased and retyped many times. The troupe consisted of six HIV-positive gay men; five looked healthy, although one had a raspy, painful voice. The sixth had horribly mottled skin, as if he had severe eczema, or perhaps Kaposi's sarcoma. He was so thin I could have lifted him as easily as I could lift an injured bird. I saw his obituary in the *New York Times* not long after the performance.

Fifteen or twenty people sat in the audience. The straights sat along the fringe of the room, while the gays occupied the center tables. We were seated beside a refined-looking heterosexual couple; across the room sat six middle-aged

women from Wisconsin who had come to the club called
"Don't Tell Mama" hoping to see female impersonators.

The dialogue was quick, humorous, sarcastic. I cried
briefly at parts, especially those that concerned family rejection. I found myself nodding too vigorously at didactic statements, worn-out, tired statements like "It's okay to kiss a
person with AIDS."

Or "I am still the same person I was before I tested HIV-
positive."

I physically strained for the stage. I had a wild desire to
stand up and proclaim my membership in this club. Had the
actors asked for a show of HIV-positive hands, I would have
gladly raised both of mine.

But they didn't.

*(I understand now that I juggled two identities that night.
On the one hand, I was an audience member watching the
actors as calmly and safely as I would observe museum
pieces or other artifacts of an extinct civilization. On the
other hand, I could easily have been that museum piece. I felt
I fit in more with the audience than with the actors, yet the
truth was that I had more in common with the men onstage
than with any of the women around me. But this is only what
I assumed; for all I knew, the room was filled with HIV-positive women just like me.*

*(Before that night I had never met anyone else with HIV
outside of Henry's office or my own home. The actors'
words, then, were the only script I had, my only example of
how other people lived with my disease.*

*(I tried to enter this script. But I bumped into a wall con-
structed of my own assumptions. I had assumed, wrongly,
that all people with AIDS spoke the same language, that we
could communicate with each other effortlessly, meaning-
fully. To some extent this is true; it is easy to talk about
symptoms and medications and insurance plans. But instead
of finding a homogeneous subculture, a group of people who*

felt exactly the same way I did, people whose lives mirrored my own, I found people very different from me. I had trouble relating. I started to realize that every infected person differs from every other infected person just as every uninfected person differs from every other.

(This is not what I expected to find.

(That night I realized I held the same stereotypes as people without AIDS. I thought I could lump all of us together and characterize us conveniently. And I believed the prevailing myths; I believed that people with AIDS were abnormal, bad, shameful.

(This was why I feared disclosure.

(Although the production was probably intended to educate the uninfected, it went a long way in educating me.

(That night I began to wish that AIDS could act as a human equalizer. That we could respect each other in a way that transcends sexual history and drug-use history and blood-use history. That future generations would see HIV not only as an intelligent, awe-inspiring virus but as the means by which the human race rediscovered its own capacity for compassion.

(I felt left out that night. I felt that I couldn't possibly suffer from AIDS as much as the men onstage must suffer; after all, I didn't have the added burden of being gay in a straight world. Now I realize that my thinking was flawed, that suffering is suffering. In our later activist work, Bill and I fought against the unspoken hierarchy of suffering that exists, a hierarchy that dictates who will receive the greatest sympathy, the most compassion. A hierarchy that separates people with AIDS into two camps: those who deserve their disease and those who do not.

(Bill and I never could think of anyone who deserved to have AIDS.)

When the show was over, the actors circulated with the audience for a few minutes; no one approached us. I suppose we looked too straight; I suppose our wedding bands cast us into that lot of young liberals who showed scholarly concern for the issue of the day. I mustered up my nerve and approached a cast member, only to have a cheery waitress clear the room for the next show. The actors dispersed.

As we waited for our car, I saw one of the actors walking slowly, head down. I yelled, "Thank you for the show!" and he looked up, nodded, and continued on his way.

If only I had said, "I have it too, I understand."

The show disturbed me. Not for what was said but for what remained unsaid. Women were absent; there was no dramatization, no acknowledgment, of the pain of forced infertility, of watching our HIV-infected partners and children die. The correct response on my part, the ethical response, would have been to offer my services as chronicler of these struggles, either as writer or actor. The minimal action should have been a letter to the producer confirming my own existence within this epidemic. But my difference made me shy and reluctant. I remained silently agitated, my concerns private, invisible, and unshared.

I know I am not alone. I'm part of a sisterhood of female partners of high-risk men, drug users, and transfusion recipients. I know there are other HIV-positive women because I know I am here, and we all cling to the apron strings of an epidemic that was supposed to pass us by. We die more quickly than our male counterparts.* We spawn diseased children for whom we cannot provide adequate care. We shout for help, but our voices are lost in the winds of ignorance and indifference. We are our generation's childbearers, but we will never bear its children.

*Recent research suggests that male and female rates of progression to AIDS are about the same. One possible explanation for the discrepancy between previous and current beliefs: in the early days of the epidemic, women were probably first diagnosed and treated at a point far along in the disease spectrum. It appeared, therefore, that HIV-positive women progressed more quickly than their male counterparts.

Disclosure

On a February morning like any other February morning I
went to work as usual, but I carried a suitcase instead of a
briefcase. I couldn't concentrate at work; I spent hours re-
arranging my desk and taking yoga breaths to quiet the shud-
dering of my heart. I repeatedly checked to see that I had my
plane tickets, irrationally fearing, perhaps even hoping, that I
had lost them. It was a gloomy day, and I grilled all new ar-
rivals to my office about the current weather situation. I
feared that rain or fog would ground my flight. Finally, tickets and clear skies confirmed, I boarded a bus to the airport
two hours earlier than necessary.

My flight wasn't smooth. The blood in my body had
ceased to flow properly; my arms were numb; my thighs tin-
gled. However, I said a silent thank-you to whoever seated
me next to the saintly nontalker who did not even flinch
when an errant AZT capsule flew onto her lap. The rain

started en route and was a compassionless storm by the time we touched down. My destination was a friend's home in Virginia, the site of an impromptu reunion between me and my three closest college friends.

A mysterious force orchestrated the circumstances of that weekend. I had begun seeing a psychologist two months earlier, as I was fraying at the corners and sinking into depression. The doctor was friendly and reputedly a good therapist. However, I was her first AIDS case; my need to blurt out the news and get on with my life—quickly—chafed against her psychoanalytic technique. Sharing my diagnosis with her felt the same as sharing it with a faceless counselor on a hot line: no personal risks, no substantial emotional exchanges. The therapist could not act as a proxy for my sequestered friends and family. I had been twenty-four months shrouded: impregnable, untouchable.

Although I had stopped seeing the therapist, I still couldn't escape the resolute voice inside that brutally pursued me. It's time, it's time, the voice said. I was paralyzed by thoughts of rejection: my world would be turned inside out, its seams ripped. Memories of my college days invaded my mind; I knew I must tell my friends if I ever expected to quiet my mind-buzzings.

The beginning of the month would be best; I wanted no more delays. I spent hours thinking of a viable and vague reason to give for my sudden urge to visit. We had rarely all been together since graduation and were now scattered across the country. By revealing I had something important to tell, I could have guaranteed everyone's attendance, but I would also have lost my option not to tell if the atmosphere didn't feel right.

I couldn't shake the feeling that I must see them. Soon. But how could I accomplish a reunion so quickly without exciting any suspicions?

As it turned out, I couldn't come up with a satisfactory

reason. So I simply decided to demand that we get together, and let the rest sort itself out. But I never even got that far. I received an intriguing phone call within two days of my musing. I was summoned to Virginia to meet with my former college buddies—no boyfriends, no husbands—during the first weekend in February. No excuses would be accepted.

None were given.

This trip was to be my dress rehearsal, my method of practicing my lines before facing my toughest audience: my parents. I needed to tell my story, but I needed to tell it first to the women with whom I had walked arm in arm along Capitol Hill and to whom I felt comfortable saying "I love you" often and publicly. I knew my carefully packaged secret could be opened safely in their presence.

We got together that weekend, and it was as if we were back in college. We spent all of Friday night reminiscing, singing Carole King songs, and eating nachos heaped with guacamole. The next morning we sat around the table and drank pot after pot of coffee and devoured junk food. For some reason the topic of AIDS kept emerging: first in reference to a *Washington Post* article; next in a crude joke about a mutual acquaintance.

Finally, when all that remained was coffee swill and doughnut crumbs, I said, "I have something really important to tell you. It's about me and Bill."

"Are you getting divorced?" one friend quickly asked.

I looked down and shook my head. "I've been keeping a secret," I said. "I'm sick. I mean, *we're* sick," I stumbled. But it was too late to turn back.

"Bill and I tested HIV-positive two years ago."

Silence then, and a blackness so complete it was like standing in a subway station during a power failure.

Then sputters of "What? What?" and instant unrelenting tears. My friends clustered around my chair, knelt on the floor, touched me wherever and however they could. I felt as if I had stabbed their very hearts, and their tears were like blood that wet my hands, my face, my lap, in a still life of pure agony.

I don't remember how long we sat there, entwined as if our lives, or at least *my* life, depended on it.

We eventually rose and cleaned the kitchen and ourselves, tried to reimpose some order on our bodies and our environment. Several times we abandoned our chores, reconvened, and simply looked at each other.

"I don't want you to die!" one of my friends would cry, and we all rehuddled again, with me as quarterback, spewing forth platitudes and reassurances until we felt strong enough to face the task of getting dressed.

I have forgotten many of the details of that weekend. I know we went to one of our favorite haunts. Although we normally would have closed the place down, we left early. What we used to do for fun just didn't seem like fun that night.

The only relic of that weekend is a photograph. In it, the four of us sit on the couch, our faces white, our eyes red, our arms around each other.

I remembered that picture, that feeling of loving arms around me, when, two months later, I told my mother I was stopping by after work to discuss something important. Bill did not come with me; I'd convinced him that my parents would be more comfortable expressing their feelings without him. Actually, I was afraid my father would go after Bill, who, at five feet four inches would have been no match for an ex-marine. Tonight, then, I would take the blows for him, at least verbally.

The day dragged on; everything I did seemed difficult. When I departed the commuter train in the Bronx that evening, I was only a few blocks away from opening the door on a new and uncertain life, and closing the door on a safe and comfortable one.

My legs felt heavy and ineffective. My parents' apartment is in a two-family house at the top of a long hill. As I walked from the train station, this hill loomed insurmountably. The stairs leading to my parents' front door are also unusually steep, so steep it is necessary to cling to the handrail just for safety's sake. When I climbed the stairs that evening, it was as if I crawled on my hands and knees to them, their baby.

The family dog greeted me as usual, and my mother had hot water for tea waiting in the carafe I had given her for Christmas. As usual.

My father paced.

I felt sick.

After accepting a cup of tea and refusing my mother's endless supply of chocolate cookies, I began.

"I have something to tell you," I said. "It's the hardest thing I'll ever have to tell you in my life."

"You've had an abortion," said my father, the Catholic deacon.

I laughed shortly. Where did *that* come from? I wondered.

"No, nothing like that," I said. "I wish it was that easy.

"There's no other way to say it than just to say it," I sputtered as I clutched the table's edge, feeling that I was babbling like an infant.

"Bill and I both have HIV."

I remember a moment of utter silence followed by my mother crying: "My baby! My baby!"

Then came the words, a frantic search for facts, comfort, anything to chase away the specter of a dying daughter who had appeared without warning at their dining room table.

Did my mother ever let go of my hand that night, and were those tears on my father's cheeks? Through all the words that followed, the subject of how I was infected never arose.

(*And my parents have never once accused Bill of murdering their daughter; have never, in fact, treated him any dif-*

ferently, any less lovingly, than the day they first welcomed him into the family in 1985.

(I know my parents probably sometimes feel embarrassed about having a daughter with AIDS. But if they are, they never let me see it. They suspended judgment and chose to respond with loyalty. AIDS has been an easier road to travel with them at my side.

(AIDS is the second scariest thing that could ever happen to me.

(The first would be to lose the love of my family.)

How many people with HIV can say that their parents never pointed a finger, never voiced shame, never for a moment asked, "How could you fail me like this?" My parents did none of these things.

I tried to strike a balance that night between optimism and realism. I told my parents about Henry and his intelligence and devotion. I told them about new drugs for HIV-related opportunistic infections. But I also told them that a cure was still probably ten years in the future, that we could only pray I'd still be here at the turn of the century to reap its benefit.

"You'd better be here," my father said, panic in his eyes.

I'll try, Daddy.

I'll try to be here for the cure.

I'll try to stay alive for you.

Heartened, fortified, I told the rest of my family. I told my sister Dolores first, a few months before her wedding. She had asked me to be a bridesmaid, and I feared that my recent bout with peripheral neuropathy would show when I walked down the aisle. The neuropathy affected my feet, legs, and hands. It is a painful nerve disease that sometimes makes walking difficult. Neuropathy burns and crackles; the pain of neuropathy can make me literally gasp when it hits. I thought it unlikely that I could successfully hide this condition on

Dolores's wedding day. *(Actually it turned out to be a good day. I walked as smoothly and gracefully as the other bridesmaids, and danced all night long.)*

Dolores's initial reaction to my call was to think that Bill and I were splitting up. Her response upon learning the truth was typical of subsequent family reactions: she was shocked; she couldn't believe this could happen; she asked why I had waited so long to say anything.

(I'm so accustomed to the presence of AIDS in my life that I'm astonished that others are still surprised by it. I have not met a person yet who is blasé when I tell them Bill and I are infected. I suppose we do not look like "AIDS"; we don't look emaciated, frail, diseased. Although we don't look the part, we are the part.)

(How obvious it is that the parts are ill-defined to begin with.)

I took Dolores with me to Henry's; she scrupulously watched everything he did, then grilled him relentlessly: What's going to happen? Why isn't there a cure? What can you do to help? What can I do to help?

The family reeled, then responded. Soon almost everyone in our immediate world knew the facts behind our secret. We have yet to experience the rejection I most feared, the isolation I thought must result. In the midst of living in what could be considered the most unfortunate of situations, I sometimes feel I am the luckiest woman alive.

Instead of being torn apart, the seams that held together the material of my world were reinforced, the tiny holes that invaded the fabric of family instantly rewoven with the thread of one disclosure.

Anamorphosis

Sometimes in the middle of an ordinary innocuous conversation—a conversation about a current movie, perhaps, or the price of gas—I want to reach over and shake my companion, and scream, "Don't you notice anything different about me?" Or, "How can you honestly think that nothing has changed?"

But of course nobody notices the change or the difference, because I've worked so hard to conceal them. And all my hard work means that I straddle two worlds: my professional, social world, where I act outwardly normally despite abnormal cells, and my other, more personal world, where abnormality predominates and the normal things of life must adapt. It is a matter of shifting weight from one foot to the other and back again. But how long before shifting becomes too exhausting, before the tireless quest for balance is finally surrendered?

AIDS is something I try to conceal like a blemish. So far, successfully. Like the best makeover from an expensive salon, it is hard to tell merely by looking what is natural and what is contrived. "Does she or doesn't she?" the old commercial asked. But that's right; this commercial was about hair coloring, not AIDS.

AIDS is like smile lines or spidery creases at the corners of your eyes: you can do your best to fill them in or plump them out, but ultimately nature exposes all. One morning you gaze in the mirror and the lines are simply there and will never go away again. One day AIDS shows itself, and it feels as if it always existed.

Anamorphosis: the deliberate distortion of an image so that it can be accurately viewed only from certain angles or with special instruments. Think of the optical illusions in psychology books: look at the picture one way and there's a vase; look at it another way and two profiles appear. Look at them one way and they are a normal, healthy couple. Look at them in another light and they are barren and afflicted. Two parts of the same picture, neither one more true than the other, each just a matter of perspective. Am I simply waiting, during my random conversations, for the angle to magically shift, the truth to be revealed?

Or must I, instead, provide the tools of discovery, tools that may be no more than the words "I have AIDS"?

I know why I am reluctant to put on my HIV face for the world. I fear that by doing so, I will make it forever my primary face. I fear that others will start addressing the sick part of me exclusively, forgetting that underneath this outer layer of AIDS is the real me, the old me, the other me, the me I still think of as me.

In fact, it has happened already. The few people who know the truth about me search my face for a picture of disease personified. Their eyes invade my skin better than any scalpel and bore under the surface of my words for some greater meaning, some key by which to reveal the sickness they now know is there. I see this in my mother's face, especially when I drone on endlessly about my job or my leaky ceiling or some other triviality. Although she murmurs appropriate assurances, I sense she does not really listen; her eyes probe to find the essence of the daughter she so willingly carried but whose life will nevertheless be so unwillingly aborted.

Disease causes a slippery slide into childhood and makes us readopt old roles. Disease makes us want to cling to our mother's hand in a crowded store or drink the hot chocolate only she could prepare when we were sick. Disease catapults us back to those days when we weren't expected to discern our own identities, when it was acceptable for adults to decipher who we really were. It is like a Halloween when I was about six or seven, one of those Halloweens when I donned a plastic Snow White face, the one that never quite provided enough air through its mouth-hole. Despite knowing precisely who I was, adults on my trick-or-treat route persisted in addressing me only as a fictitious character: "Oh, how precious. But where are your little friends, the dwarves?"

It was an irritating charade, and I was anxious then, as I find myself anxious now, to hurry home and take off my self-imposed mask.

Recently I began dreaming about losing my teeth, sometimes one by one, sometimes in groups of five or ten. They crumble like squeezed fistfuls of dry dirt, filling my mouth painfully, making me choke. Not only do my teeth fail me, but bridges, braces, and other fabricated retainers of beauty snap like chewed ice. In my dreams, not only the foundations, but also the reinforcements fall. I have heard that to dream of losing teeth is to dream of losing control. It is quite possible that I dream about losing the person I once was. It is also possible that my dreams actually tell me to do what I know I must do: to purposely lose control and stop this deliberate deception.

I will listen to my dreams, then, and unmask. And through unmasking, retain those who cherish the exposed part of me. Discard, like old pretenses, those who prefer me carefully concealed. But in either case I must remember the law of physics, that energy is neither created nor destroyed; it just changes form. The burden of dishonesty lifted from my shoulders will become the burden of honesty imposed elsewhere. In the future I may see little difference between my image and the faces of new confidantes.

After all, it is only natural that a little bit of me should rub off on them.

Notes On a Few Infected Women

Only five of us showed up, including one other new member. Two black, three white, two married, initial diagnoses ranging from three years to six months ago. One woman infected since 1981, who attributes her continuing health to a West Indian root, brewed into a tea and taken cold, like soda.

It was my first visit to a support group, and I wanted to blurt out my story, but surrendered to the assertiveness of the other new member. Sheila, diagnosed two years ago, suffers from severe swelling of her glands; she now wears long wigs to keep people from asking if she has the mumps. She uses a variety of traditional and nontraditional therapies, from AZT to acupuncture. She's undergoing radiation treatment, which shrinks her swollen nodes but which also makes her parched. Her speech is rather slow and punctuated by her efforts to produce saliva. Recently she's experienced hearing loss from the swelling. To the rest of us, her glands appear unremarkable, unnoticeable. She nonetheless perceives them as huge.

(*I remember a similar feeling when I had HIV-related seborrheic dermatitis. I was so horrified by the sight of my blistered skin, so paranoid at the thought of being stared at, that I couldn't believe that my skin looked fine even after the condition cleared. How brave that "AIDS Alive" actor was to get up in front of an audience with his mottled, painful-looking skin.*)

Eleanor is a suburban mother, a person you'd likely encounter at the mall. She refuses traditional medicine and speaks extensively about the many alternative healing groups she attends. In fact, going to these various meetings, sometimes several on any given day, seems to occupy the majority of her time.

(*But when does she stop talking about how to live and actually do the living? I thought.*)

Anger, venom even, when she recalls learning that her husband had a number of secret homosexual affairs while she worked to put him through school. Anger at his deception, anger at herself for trusting him. Fear at the thought of her children's reaction to her disease, but most especially their reaction to its original source in their lives.

(*But these children will have to watch their father die, I thought, and he will still be their father, despite his affairs, regardless of how he became sick.*

(*In the end, does it really matter "how"?*)

Eleanor appealed to me as the other married member of the group: Did you stop having sex? Should I divorce him because he doesn't believe in my healing methods? Because he did this to me? We discussed using condoms even with HIV-positive partners, not to prevent pregnancy, but to keep away the virus. I was the only one there not practicing safe sex, considering such practices for me to be several years too late.

(*I didn't share their concerns. It seemed redundant to*

erect barriers after the fact. Some people will argue that you can accumulate more virus if you have unprotected sex with an infected partner. But the amount of new virus you'd actually encounter is infinitesimal. As Henry says, it would have as much effect as giving a penny to a millionaire.

(I suppose practicing safe sex could still have some medical benefit, could still conceivably prevent the transmission of other infections. But by this time, I was already positive for all known transmissable agents such as cytomegalovirus and hepatitis B. Besides, I didn't feel I could ever catch anything worse than HIV.)

Then there was Carole, infected through a contaminated needle-stick while on the job. I did not care for her; she was brittle, edgy. She talked about her intractable junk-food habit in a way that made me feel silly about my own nutritional concerns.

(She looked to me as if she was posing. But maybe her feelings about nutrition were similar to my feelings about safe sex.)

Carole is hell-bent on revenge against her employer, whom she considers directly responsible for her condition.

(She looked awfully healthy, though. Perhaps some people thrive on anger.)

So there I was, in a group specifically for non-drug-abusing HIV-positive women, but feeling more isolated than before I walked into the room. I felt pierced and stung by their anger against men, against institutions, against God, against randomness, against reality. Maybe I'm just ignorant, or hopelessly naive, yet I can't help but think: I have a happy marriage, wonderful friends and family, an excellent doctor, and a growing sense of urgency to live in the present without regret.

Anger is too time-consuming, and I don't feel I have time to waste.

Maybe I was in the wrong place at the wrong time.

I never went back to that group again.

Irene's Gift

I felt an undeniable—and shameful—rush of satisfaction. She had been, after all, a prostitute and crack-head for three years, had sold herself for drugs right up until the time she delivered her second child five months ago. Residents of her neighborhood spit at her when she passed, a disgusting addict who didn't give a shit about her baby's health but only wanted to feel that expansive high, even if it meant fondling some syphilis-laden man.

We sat in her sterile room on the locked psychiatric ward. I had been sent there as part of my job as a behavioral researcher to write down her story, to provide a human vignette to flesh out the impersonal statistics we collected. The depravity of her life couldn't be exaggerated: a drug-dealer mother; nine addicted siblings who sold themselves to fill their pipes; a husband who once shot her; no money; skin and bones; no one to turn to except, in her eyes, God.

I kept thinking, she's got to have AIDS. Wishing, yes, *wishing,* that she did, so I could nod and act unsurprised but compassionate, all the while thinking, "Well, what did you expect?"

I listened to an hour of circular stories, each nauseating, tearing.

Then Irene said, "My second test was negative yesterday. It must've been a gift from the Lord, because I was sure I had got the AIDS."

Two Years

Still here two years later.

We managed our first two years with few problems—a bad case of strep, several flus, but no pneumonia, Kaposi's sarcoma, or even a hospitalization between us. My parents know we're HIV-positive. Bill told his mother but not his father; she wants to tell him herself when she thinks he can handle it. It is six months later, and he still doesn't know.

We survived Christmas of 1989, the original target date given when we pushed and pulled Henry for a prediction. When it became apparent that we'd be around to celebrate this holiday, we gave Henry an electronic crystal ball and an extra set of batteries to assist him with future forecasting.

Two years have passed since our diagnoses; we are still here, but we are no longer the same.

I've been officially diagnosed with a mild case of peripheral neuropathy, characterized by pain in my legs, feet, and hands and a concurrent loss of strength—walking up a flight of stairs definitely makes me grimace. I'm slower, a lumbering, grazing cow, the old lady you get caught behind on the subway stairs as the doors of your train close. I am, however, still walking, and still working.

Although not insufferably debilitating, the neuropathy was bad enough to warrant a trip to a specialist, who put electrodes on my arms and legs and administered shock to test the speed of my nerve reactions. My response strayed from the norm—not too much, but just enough to explain my recent pain. The doctor, whose insensitivity could not be measured, said I shouldn't worry yet: I won't die until my numbers fall a little lower on his machine. He then asked when I planned to have children, despite his knowing my HIV status. Tongue-tied, I stammered that I didn't think I'd ever have children. He winked and nudged me with his elbow, saying that I was still young and should realize that nature has a way of deciding these things for you.

Henry looked at the findings, told me to think about high-dose steroid therapy; prednisone used in a pulsing pattern could help keep the pain and inflammation under control. Henry also said he doesn't think I'm on my way out. Our code for talking prognosis is to discuss vacations; he promised to let me know when the end is near by telling me to plan those long-dreamed-about trips to faraway places. Tonight he told me not to get out the brochures just yet.

So there's nothing I can do at this moment, except be thankful that so far my neurological manifestations of AIDS have been peripheral. I'm not an incontinent mute, unable to respond to stimuli, unable to even care about not responding. Exercise won't help me, or hurt me. My neuropathy will either progress or recede according to its own will, and despite mine.

I think I'm supposed to be frightened at this development, but I'm not. I've known for months that something was wrong, and I've known for a year that I'm no longer asymptomatic. Henry gently shares the results of studies showing that HIV-positive women decline more quickly than their male counterparts. It is a trend Bill and I appear to substantiate, and is one of those facts that Henry presents as a challenge, scientifically, without sentiment:

Will you be part of the normal curve, or will you be an outlier?

I want desperately to be an outlier, but I don't know whether this is possible. My heart says one thing; science says another.

I was born on the first Saturday of August 1963, at Flower Fifth Avenue Hospital overlooking Central Park. My mother labored for over twenty-four hours, and the umbilical cord was wrapped around my neck. It was a rough start. Apparently there were two of me at one time, but my twin never fully developed. I am sorry this happened; had my twin survived, at least my mother might have been comforted after my death by the child who shared the same womb with me. My mother floated in the solace of Demerol for days after my birth, and saw pink bunnies hopping among the roses in her bedside vase. She still remembers how happy they looked.

My family long occupied the apartment building where I spent most of my childhood. My parents moved from a three-room on the third floor to a six-room on the fourth when their third child was born. Over the years, other family members also lived in the building: my aunt and uncle and cousins; my grandmother; my great-grandmother; my great-uncle. My sister Maureen and her husband moved into a fifth-floor apartment when George finished his tour of duty in Vietnam. That was the norm in my neighborhood: pieces of families lived on the same block, or in the same building, mothers and daughters and granddaughters separated only by a flight of stairs.

I am the youngest of four children. Almost sixteen years separate me from my oldest sister. Besides Maureen, the oldest, I have a brother, Stephen, born in 1950, and a sister, Dolores, who is six years older than I. I never really got to know Maureen and Steve until we all were adults. And although Dolores and I were closer in age, the six-year difference was enough to keep us from becoming friends.

Although the four children never played together, we preserved our solidarity as a family on the roof of our apartment building. Four sets of initials are dug side by side into the tar around the chimney: MOR, SOR, DOR, JOR. We carefully captured the legacy of the O'Reilly children in a place we never occupied together, but where we nonetheless found each other generation after generation.

Maureen taught me to do my first dance, the slide. She was a member of the drill team in high school and practiced her moves at home using a green plastic rifle. She attended a city college as an art major, but never finished because she married when she was twenty years old. Maureen was more a mother than a sister to me, and with her Barbara Feldon–style hair and her short, short dresses, she was remote and glamorous. I was five years old when she married; Dolores and I wore matching green velvet dresses to her wedding, and rings of daisies in our hair.

Steve also lived in a remote world, a world of hanging out in the school yard, of girls, parties, and work. He gave me wonderful Christmas presents: a pogo stick one year, a Hoppity-Hop the next, all to the dismay of our neighbors downstairs. He often came home at midnight laden with dozens of White Castle hamburgers, and he and my mother compan-

ionably ate them as if it were the middle of the day. Steve wore an army jacket and a headband around his long red-brown hair, but never served in Vietnam; he became deaf in one ear after falling out of a tree when he was twelve. He had a series of pretty girlfriends, including one who later became his wife. He is quiet, painfully so at times, and always seems to have trouble brewing somewhere. I remember little of my childhood with him. I do remember that he practiced his judo moves on me.

My sister Dolores and I steadfastly hated each other through childhood. I was as annoying to her as a static-filled skirt. I drew on her brand-new Baby Boo doll and hung her bra on the window guard for the whole neighborhood to see. Also, I was sickly, and this fact made me all the more pathetic in her eyes. I threw myself at her in ill-tempered rage, and she threw herself right back. Once she hit me so hard that my glasses flew out the window and landed on the fire escape.

Dolores capitalized on my weak stomach and dissected bugs in front of me, talked long and in detail about veins, and tried to convince me that, when I was born, the doctors took off the top of my head and replaced my brains with spaghetti. There were moments of solidarity over the years, however, like the time I flushed my pork chops down the toilet and she didn't tattle, and when at bedtime we sang "Good Night, Sleep Tight" from The Lawrence Welk Show *to each other. Of the four children, Dolores is the funny one, the one who can talk to anyone, the one who always says exactly what is on her mind. She is pretty, and I envied her looks in the same way I envied Maureen's. I often felt that all the beauty in my family had already been apportioned by the time I came along.*

Dolores married her first husband when she was nineteen, and it was then that we really became friends; now we talk to each other almost daily. In 1994, when Bill's intestine rup-

tured while we were on vacation, Dolores was the first per-son—in fact the only person besides Henry—whom I called. She immediately jumped in her car and made a six-hour trip alone in the middle of the night to be with me.

But she was not the only one to respond when I was stranded in a strange city with my husband near death. A day later Maureen caught a flight from Kansas City, and Steve arrived at midnight after driving north from his home in Connecticut. We all stayed in one room at a Howard Johnson's motel near the hospital, sleeping in the same space for the first time in over twenty years.

PART FOUR: 1990

Take it now, take it now
Make your heart beat faster,
Pow.

Wash the floor at 5 AM
Complete a whole day's work by 10.
No more pain, never tired
Drop 10 pounds, superwired
Pituitary going wild—

Need to rest, God help me rest
Take from me this tireless quest.
Try the couch, try the floor
Destined now to sleep no more.

Taper down, taper down
40, 20, going fast
10 to 5, then out of gas.
Legs are hurting, fingers aching
Exhausted by the last dose taken.

A whole month lost in a blurry flash.
Crash.

"Prednisone Psychosis," March 15, 1990

Fearing Cancer

The New York Times reported yesterday that people taking AZT are 48 percent more likely to develop lymphoma. Now that AIDS patients are living longer, new villains lurk in the shadows and wait to replace the first generation of assassins: *pneumocystis carinii* pneumonia and Kaposi's sarcoma.

Particularly worrisome is that this cancer strikes most often when T4 levels fall below fifty; Bill's T4 count is seventeen. T4 cells, otherwise known as T cells or CD4 cells, are immune system markers. A healthy, HIV-uninfected person would normally have about one thousand T4 cells.

Bill has lost weight recently, despite the fact that he constantly eats. Yet he eats and gets thinner and never complains. I have a horrible vision of him slipping away quietly without a word of warning. Unlike me, for I will depart in chaos and verbal incontinence.

Lymphoma really should not be so frightening. Certainly

it is no more terrifying than AIDS dementia. But AIDS is new enough to be somewhat exotic; hope for a miracle cure or a heretofore unknown progression to dormancy is still viable, if improbable. But a person with cancer almost certainly dies of cancer, at least in my world. I still hold out some hope for myself.

It's absurd to think I might actually view the manifestations of AIDS as preferable to the malignancy and cell death of cancer. It is absurd to think this, especially as the consequences of each are probably the same.

Until

August 19, 1990 _____

It began about sex, or rather the lack of it. Then all of the same old words poured out of my mouth:

Don't you care that we're frigid?

You can't keep this to yourself any longer.

It's abnormal to feel nothing.

There are people who want to help you.

And on and on and on.

Until.

I did this to you, Bill says. I don't deserve to be loved.

I felt a knife worse than neuropathy stab my heart then, saw that I, in effect, had used a knife to cut away months and years of apparent strength, to whittle down this man, this husband, to carve him like a battered child convinced he is beaten, deservedly, just for the mistake of being alive.

Like a bolt of lightning that for a brief moment illuminates so violently, I remember countless examples of my irritability and self-pity, my hostility unspoken but not unnoticed. I see my anger, anger, anger concealed behind the smile of a devoted wife. I remember moments of unlove that only confirmed his guilt, that only wove more tightly the material of his hair shirt.

Until finally the words burst from his lips, unkissed by compassion for so long:

I don't deserve to be loved.

MRI

August 23, 1990 _____

This morning Bill will have an MRI to try to determine the reason for his weight loss, his fatigue, his "twinge of a headache." Henry also recently saw five lesions in the superior nasal arcade of Bill's right eye. These need to be investigated by an ophthalmologist for possible signs of cytomegalovirus (CMV) chorioretinitis, one of the leading causes of blindness in HIV-infected people.

Bill's memory has never been outstanding, except for numbers. Bill can see a phone number once, or a twenty-digit string of computer code, and never forget it. Lately, however, he has begun to defer to me on almost every question requiring memory. He makes fun of his deficit, but I wonder if he realizes its greater implications.

While examining me last night, Henry said, "Don't look at Bill when you answer this question."

He then asked quickly, "Have you noticed any functional changes in him?"

I didn't look at Bill, couldn't look at him, really, and felt like Judas with the soldiers when I nodded.

Bill preferred to go alone for his MRI, and kept joking about "a tumor the size of Toledo." He also recited an imaginary conversation in which the technician asks him: "And what part of the body are we studying today, Mr. Burns?"

To which Bill cryptically replies, Bela Lugosi–style, "The *brain!*"

I have begun to think about life insurance policies, burial arrangements, and living wills. I am feeling guilty over any part I played in wearing down Bill's defenses over the years, either through irritability or my own chronic illness. Maybe my insistence on talking about AIDS is good for me but not for him. Maybe thinking so much about AIDS has only made Bill feel worse, has made him sick. It is clear I've failed in my quest to deflect illness away from him by taking on enough for both of us.

Maybe this morning my nerves are stretched tighter than usual and I don't want to admit that we are both losing control of our bodies.

The results of the MRI won't be in before nine-thirty. I know my mother will call me at least five times before then, as if I might forget to tell her the outcome.

Bill worked late last night and fell on the way home from the train station. That's perfectly understandable: it was pitch dark, and the path that leads to our parking lot is overgrown and littered with hundreds of rocks. All the same, the old Bill wouldn't have fallen, and I wanted to cry for the loss of Bill as I first knew him.

On Friday a voice on our answering machine said, "Your MRI was normal." On Tuesday the ophthalmologist could not locate the spots Henry had observed the previous week.

And so ends, for now, another episode of terror, leaving me jelly-kneed with relief and faintly annoyed at its anticlimax.

I still don't understand why Bill falls asleep whenever he sits down with nothing to do. It's hard to believe he is so simpleminded that being still causes him to nod off. Or is it that he needs so much extra sleep that his body greedily appropriates each available minute? He is a defective windup toy, with springs that jump efficiently to action at times, and pitch him over the table's edge at others. A few whirs, a few aborted movements, then nothing.

Mom's voice gurgled when I told her the results, and Bill's mother whispered over and over, "Oh, thank God, thank God." I felt like an imposter of love. Their grief is so much more tangible and immediate than my own. I felt jealous; they were genuinely comforted by the test results; they truly felt as if another disaster had been averted. They don't realize, or don't acknowledge, that disaster still looms. I wish I could feel that kind of relief. For Bill's sake, I wish I could put on a determinedly optimistic face and fool him into thinking I believed that everything would now be all right.

Our mothers react similarly to our illness despite their very different personalities. Perhaps they act like every mother whose child is sick or undergoing some unfixable dilemma. And they react this way: they grab onto any morsel of good news and hope it represents the entire picture. The MRI was good; that means Bill is perfectly healthy, that everything is fine, that we are allowed to pretend the disease is not progressing.

They are mothers, and they must make everything better,

they must hide the wounds under a bandage and a kiss. They must do this, and they cannot help themselves. It is what I would do if I were a mother; I would do anything to keep my child from pain, were it psychological or physical. This is how I would feel if I were a mother. But I am not a mother.

Sometimes I want to shake them out of their delusions and say, "It is not all right. You cannot make it right simply by saying it is."

This seems unnecessarily cruel, so I remain quiet and keep my honesty to myself.

I cannot believe I wanted the MRI to reveal an abnormality, but I can believe I wanted an answer by which to formulate a response. These are the maddening aspects of HIV: indistinct fatigue with headaches, apathy, loss of spirit, concession to death. These are the realms of the soul, which cannot be revived with Naprosyn or anti-virals and whose etiology is clear but whose cure is not mine to give or receive.

Fag Hag

I first heard the term "fag hag" in 1983 at a college conference. After a long day of training my fellow students and I had gathered together to drink beer and smoke cigarettes in a lounge at DePaul University. Across the room, on a couch surrounded by most of the female students, sat Bill. Standing next to me was a good-looking guy who I think did his research in Amsterdam to take advantage of the city's legalized drugs and prostitutes. He thrust his chin toward the couch and muttered derisively, "What a bunch of fag hags."

Fag hag: a woman with a penchant for luring homosexual men to the other side. At the time I simply dismissed the comment as ignorant. Yet I never forgot it, and I remember feeling puzzled when I heard it. What did everyone else see in Bill that I did not? After all, he didn't lisp, he didn't sashay, he wasn't artistic. He was strong and confident. He didn't fit the mythological model of the gay man. But he also didn't fit any other prescribed pattern. His attraction largely lay in the way he stood apart from all the other men I knew, the way he didn't try to fit into a mold whose ridges and indentations were smoothed flat and shapeless from overuse.

He was then, and is now, a gentle blend of the qualities that are perceived to be male and female. Given a piece of wood, he'll create something both beautiful and functional. Put him in a room with a child, and he's as comfortable playing cops and robbers as he is rocking that same child to sleep.

He is like an emerald, rich in his nuances of color, a valuable gem. A jewel whose surface looks hard and impenetrable but which is actually soft and acquiescent. Whose character is defined in part by its ability to withstand the trauma imposed by human hands.

I have never been attracted to aggressive men, men who throw their sex and their disdain into your face as sharply and brutally as they would snap a wet towel in a locker room. Prior to Bill, my boyfriends were all artists or writers or musicians in some form; none of them were macho or particularly tough. I heard that one of them later came out of the closet. I remember disliking one boyfriend when he started working out and wanting me to be more like the women he saw in pornographic magazines. Over the years I had plenty of flirtations as well, the most significant of which involved a man who was openly gay, but who nonetheless seemed interested in stretching his own boundaries a little.

Fag hag?

Perhaps it is true. Perhaps this is how I should be characterized. It is easy for me to understand why I feel this way: I am afraid of large men, of physically intimidating men, of men who could whip me around like a yarn doll simply because it is possible.

And this is why I am afraid:

Long before it became popular to do so, I remembered

some repressed memories. Through adolescent dreams, through random flashes to a long-ago day, the source of my fear and my need for a gentle man became clear. It is a flash only, of pearl-pink tiles cold and unyielding under my head, of a toilet's silver pipe mimicking the curve of my spine as I crouched and hid. I think I was about five years old, or younger, and I know I was in someone else's home, not my own. I remember that my mouth felt as if I'd eaten salty crackers without milk to wash them down. Above me was a face, but my mind's defense system, or perhaps God's mercy, has blurred it so that it is now unrecognizable.

When I reinterpret this moment in light of my pre-adolescent night-dreams, often marked by sexual torture, I can surmise what happened. I never told my parents or anyone else of this event; I think I probably wanted to, but dreaded their reaction, feared I would be blamed. Perhaps if I had told them, I wouldn't have been plagued by the following recurring nightmare:

My sister Dolores and I follow my parents across a bridge, which splits in two. Our section sinks into the water, and my sister and I cry out for help and flounder against the tide. We open our mouths, but our screams cannot be heard over the roar of the water. Our parents reach the safety of the shore, never knowing what terror has beset their daughters.

So I am left with this thought: perhaps it is true, perhaps I am a fag hag, and with good reason. But at least I am a happy hag, at least I am loved and do not fear that my body will be pierced and my soul trashed by a huge, angry man. At least I can say that the only hand raised around me is the one raised to pull me to safety, to rescue me when I fall into the water.

Anchor

She is someone who has gone too far, a friend whose actions I no longer fathom.

She is funny and brilliant, an incisive writer with a quick wit and an easiness of personality that makes her equally comfortable at a meat-market bar or an opening-night gala. Blatantly sexual almost to the point of nonchalance, she always smoked too much, drank to excess, and did recreational drugs too often. I thought she would settle down after college. But instead she replaced pub nights with happy hours; replaced schoolboys with suited businessmen. Then I told her I had AIDS; me, the quiet friend, the one sickeningly monogamous, the one occasionally called a prude by guys who weren't lucky.

After learning about me, my friend thought about being tested, but I don't think she ever was. She continued to have unprotected sex with men of unknown histories as if she never had a friend with AIDS.

I love you, I love you. Why don't you love yourself?

And I see her repeating my own life and my own choices. I see her embracing death and spiraling downward, and I want to kill her for her delusions and wrap her under my coat and protect her from herself. But this reaction is like that of a mother who wants to shelter her child from the world, who wants to keep her child from making the same mistakes, who wants her own experiences and suffering to benefit the person she loves most.

But I cannot be her mother; I can only be her friend.

Yet I still think: You're watching me die and you're reaching for the same anchor as it passes on its way to the ocean's floor. You're reaching for an anchor that will not stabilize you, but will take you to the depths of despair.

I can't save you.

It appears I never knew how to swim.

Waiting for the Bloodletting

September 6, 1990

We all sit, adults with a decidedly grown-up disease, on
hard plastic chairs and overly soft couches, gazing now and
again at the toy box filled with well-worn dolls and chewed-
upon books, or at the bulletin board covered with pictures of
the children being treated for chicken pox by the same man
who monitors our T cells. It is Wednesday night, nine
o'clock, and most of us have been sitting here since six.

I am always too warm or too cold here, but it is hard to tell
whether the thermostat needs adjusting or I have a fever. The
walls are the color of baby cough medicine, bright artificial
sunshine, like a van Gogh painting. Michelle walks back and
forth, back and forth, jabbering incessantly: she has not taken
her methadone today. She wears tight blue jeans ripped at the
knees and high leather boots; her hair hangs down to her
waist, and she has perfect features and skin the color of wet
sand. She is as beautiful as any fashion model, but hardly as

serene. She turns to me and says she is pregnant; I smile and say "Congratulations," but I don't believe her. I think she just fantasizes.

She wasn't fantasizing. Six months later she gave birth to a healthy baby. By healthy, I mean, of course, that she had an HIV-free baby who needed only to be detoxed in his first few days.

There is another woman here, whose thread-thin braid trails on the floor as she stretches across two chairs, legs up, cane loosely held in one hand. We do not speak, although she was here the night of my first visit. She is the first woman with HIV that I knowingly encountered. She makes me nervous, not because of anything she has done or said but because she is obviously unwell; she represents my future. We watch each other with eyes lowered and heads averted as one or the other ventures to the bathroom: who is more unsteady tonight? I don't think she works anymore, and my tailored clothes and commuter sneakers feel too smug. I close my eyes in feigned sleep.

A number of new patients dot the room. Some I will see over and over again as the months and years pass; some will disappear as instantly as spooned sugar in a cup of coffee. Collectively, our stomachs growl with missed dinners, and our bones and chair legs creak as we reposition ourselves for the duration. The phone rings, and we shamelessly listen, constructing crises worse than our own from the one-sided narratives we hear.

Then, singly, or sometimes in pairs, we unfold and clear the waiting room, shoes removed for the weigh-in, arms extended for the bloodletting.

I first learned about death in the second grade, when my friend Melissa died of leukemia.

Melissa lived on the first floor of my building. She was a year ahead of me in school and had coppery hair clasped in a large barrette at the back of her head. She had clear green eyes and the same space between her front teeth that all children seem to have at that age. Melissa was all wrists and knees and elbows, her body a set of protrusions that would have been awkward had she ever reached adolescence. Delicate, she rarely went outside, and her mother allowed only certain of the neighborhood children into her room to play. I was one of the chosen few, probably because I was quiet and well mannered, a child who would not stress Melissa physically or emotionally.

I liked Melissa. The other kids thought her spoiled and coddled, because she always had the newest toys, and plenty of them. I never felt jealous; rather I felt privileged on those days I visited her. She was not what the other children said she was; she was not a child who thought herself better than us. She was a perfectly normal little girl who liked to play jacks and old maid, who was soft-spoken and smiled a lot, who was, in fact, never pushy or bossy at all, at least not toward me. She was my friend.

Every morning my mother stood at my bedroom window and watched me walk to school. She also watched Melissa. My mother knew, as all the mothers knew, that Melissa was sick. She watched her laboriously make her way each morning; she watched her stop every few steps, put down her bookbag, and catch her breath. I don't remember Melissa doing this; perhaps I was so used to it that it no longer seemed unusual. I knew Melissa was frail, but that was just another one of her traits, like her green eyes and the gap between her teeth. I never thought about it, never realized that she couldn't go on forever living the way she did, within the walls of her apartment, comforted by her collection of toys.

Melissa's middle name was Ann, like my own, and spelled the same way, no e on the end. I felt this bound us together somehow. We both had curly red hair, another important link to a seven-year-old. I don't know what else we had in common—spelling tests, socks that fell down when we walked, pencil boxes, maybe—but I guess it was enough, because I still remember her.

One morning in late September 1970, the principal made an announcement over the loudspeaker. She said that one of our third graders had died that morning. She then asked us to pray for Melissa and for her family; she asked us to ask God to forgive Melissa's sins and welcome her into his kingdom.

Stunned, I didn't know what to do. But I knew I should do something; I knew I should mourn in some way. The teacher asked us to bow our heads, and I leaned my forehead on my desk and licked the tissue that I held perpetually in my hand.

*There, I thought, everyone will think I'm crying and that's
good, because that's what you're supposed to do when
you're sad.*

I didn't actually cry until I arrived home for lunch that
day. I walked up the four flights of stairs, walked into the
apartment as I always did at eleven forty-five, looked at
my mother, and sank to my knees, crying, "Melissa's
dead!"

I curled up on the turquoise shag rug in the foyer and
sobbed. My mother, hearing the news for the first time, and
apparently not having noticed when she looked out the window that morning that Melissa wasn't there, watched me fall,
then ran into the bathroom to compose herself.

Where did you go? I thought, feeling as if I were alone in
the world.

But my mother returned in an instant, her eyes moist, her
shoulders squared, and she knelt with me on the shag rug
and let me cry.

We went to Melissa's funeral Mass, and I misbehaved with
another little girl, talking and fidgeting, acutely aware of
why I was there, but unwilling to give the ritual my attention.

I talked with Melissa regularly after she died; I thought
her vantage point from the afterlife was the corner of my
bedroom ceiling. A year or two later, Melissa's mother became pregnant. She was due in the summer, and I prayed
and prayed that the baby would arrive on my birthday. I
wanted a sign that Melissa still thought about me, a sign that
she wasn't really gone completely. On the first of August, I
woke up to birthday wishes and presents. In my excitement, I
forgot what else I had wished for that day.

"By the way," my mother said, up to her elbows in dish-
water, "Melissa's mother had her baby this morning. A little
girl."

On that summer's day I truly believed that death was a
transformation and not an end. That even long-deceased

friends could make their presence known in strange and miraculous ways.

I went into my room that birthday morning and looked up at the corner of my ceiling, and I smiled.

Sometimes I still do.

PART FIVE: 1991

The woman has not just one death to fear, although she herself is going to die just once and for all; she has not just one soul to be anxious about, although she herself has only one. Rather, she trembles on behalf of her children, she trembles for their families, the women and the children, and by as much as the root extends itself into many shoots, by that much are her anxieties more than sufficient for her. And in the case of each of these relatives, one of them will either sustain a loss, or a bodily illness, or some other undesirable accident; necessity makes us disconsolate and mournful no less than the victims themselves. If everyone dies before her, the sorrow is intolerable, but if those remain while others are carried away by untimely deaths, she does not in this way find a pure consolation.

Saint John Chrysostom, fourth century

PART FIVE 1991

War Zone

April 24, 1991

The sun rises over the Hudson River in a reluctant, foggy way; the George Washington Bridge still hides within the outlines of the Bronx. It is my second full day of hospitalization, and my second hospitalization in less than six weeks. Two separate opportunistic infections, neither yet resolved. I have entered the age of AIDS.

My left side is a war zone. Lesions on my ear and face—painful, disgusting, oozy—spread, ripping my vanity to shreds. A lump on my left hip, removed and studied: apparently *mycobacterium avium intracellulare*. More lumps, now moving to the right side. A newly acquired cane and limp. Friends with newly acquired looks of fear and pity. Am I so stupid that I haven't realized I'm dying? Or is everyone else just overreacting?

I like the fact that two of the drugs in my treatment regimen are used for leprosy. I should hang a bell around my neck, take my carefully isolated hospital cup in hand, and crawl along the eighth floor corridor crying, "Unclean! Unclean!" But I won't. How lucky I am that I'm not relegated to an unsanitary cave for the duration of my existence, that I'm sitting in a private room watching the sun rise.

I sat by the window to think and pray, but as usual, the former got in the way of the latter. Fears cloud my prayers this morning. Fears about my face never clearing, about leaving Bill behind or Bill leaving me behind. Fears about the effects of all of these drugs on my body. Fears about finances and funeral arrangements. These fears make me crazy and tired.

My prayer for this morning, then, should be:

Let me give my fears about my illness, and my illness itself, into your keeping, because my fears are more than I can handle on my own.

Unthinkable Things

The unthinkable has happened, and so quickly.

Those tiny lesions in Bill's eyes, appearing briefly and disappearing last August, reemerged in January: cytomegalovirus infection, or CMV. Their reappearance resulted in a two-week hospitalization, during which a catheter was surgically implanted in Bill's chest so that he could receive daily doses of a chemotherapy drug called Cytovene. He is in the hospital again, as I write, with a staph infection. His six-month-old catheter, contaminated, had to be removed; its replacement will be inserted on Wednesday—that is, it will be if his gallium scan does not reveal *pneumocystis carinii* pneumonia (he has a dry cough and fevers), and his CAT scan does not reveal lymphoma (he has a hard lump in front of his left ear). He now must decide whether to go out on permanent disability; his job was recently restructured to allow him to work at home the majority of his time.

Appropriately, his job title was changed to senior internal consultant, or SIC.

I am on short-term disability leave at the moment, having been hospitalized twice in the last six months. Henry believes I may have tuberculosis manifested in an unprecedented way: pea-sized lumps on my arms and legs, lesions on my left ear and cheek. I am finally on the right cocktail of medications, or so we think, and I hope to return to work soon. The last of the facial scabs fell off this afternoon, and for the first time in months I can look in the mirror without flinching.

We moved into a beautiful new place in January, with cathedral ceilings, a soaring stone fireplace, and wraparound deck, all set within a veritable forest. It is the house of my fantasies: secluded, light-filled, with a family of deer that appear on the lawn and munch the bushes every evening. Two weeks after we moved in, Bill was hospitalized; since then we've barely spent a full month here together. My Catholic school upbringing tempts me to believe that God punishes us for being greedy, for wanting too much too soon, for not saving for that proverbial rainy day.

My more secular side counters: If not now, when?

And what are these days if not rainy?

I thought the end would be more sudden, more agonizing. Rather, it's gradual, invasive, a subtle whittling away of function and strength, as slow as an IV drip into a tired vein, as unglamorous as a piece of dry toast at breakfast.

Torture

I don't feel lucky, despite what Henry says. I'm tired of putting on the brave face, being noble in adversity, acting the tireless warrior, trying to project all those qualities that are supposed to define the terminally ill. If I am to be an invalid, let me be an invalid; if I'm to be whole, let me be whole. Too many shades of gray crowd and cloud my mind; too many almost-recoveries fling me into oblivion.

Some days, this day, I just want to get on with it, the dying. Living is so tortuous at times, and not only because of physical pain, which at the moment is mercifully absent. The torture comes with unpredictability to an unprecedented degree. The torture comes in the faces of family and friends, in their pity and their sorrow, in their inability to remember the person I was before I became sick. The torture comes in unrealized potentials, unconceived babies, a limping approach to age thirty.

Living Death

She is not the first person I've known to commit suicide, but she is the first HIV-positive person I've known to kill herself.

Barbara did it right on her second attempt.

I found out last night. I suspect she died of an overdose of the drugs that ruled so much of her life. After her first attempt a couple of months ago, she spent time in an inpatient psychiatric ward, but apparently not enough time. Or perhaps no amount of therapy, no treatment plan, would have been enough to save her.

I last saw Barbara in May, when she came to a support group meeting stoned to the stratosphere, wearing a skintight yellow skirt. I met her in the bathroom, gazing at herself in the full-length mirror. She clung to me as a sympathetic sister-in-arms.

"All men want is your cunt," she said. "They don't care

about you, they make promises they don't keep. They only want one thing."

She paced and shouted on those cold tiles, and I later told Bill that I thought she teetered on the edge of sanity. In that bathroom on that spring day, in her sleazy, eye-riveting outfit, she was a thrashing ball of rage and pain.

Barbara's toddler died of AIDS last year; she had transmitted the virus to him at birth. I am told she killed herself on the first anniversary of his death.

Perhaps this was the only way she felt she could commemorate such an event.

In Barbara I saw the deep caldera of anguish that so often accompanies, and sometimes overshadows, the physical manifestations of AIDS. Barbara's HIV infection had not yet caused the deterioration of her body, but her soul and spirit were devastated beyond repair, her ability to fight as compromised as the immunity of a person in the final stages of disease.

Barbara was a mother who loved her child and infected her child with the virus that killed him. He was part of her, and when she lost him, she lost the part of herself that had a reason to live.

(*I am not a mother; I know I will never be a mother. Yet I grieve for a child that I only imagined; I grieve for Sarah who never was. My grief might appear trivial compared to Barbara's, yet I know how my grief haunts me. I can easily imagine how Barbara's grief haunted her.*)

Perhaps in Barbara's life, her child was her only consolation. When he died, perhaps she found herself inconsolable by anyone except the child who waited for her, who had surely long forgiven her, if forgiveness and an afterlife are more than simply constructs of the fearful.

The Girl With . . .

October 9, 1991 _____

I was asthmatic as a child. Severe attacks every other week often landed me in the hospital. I missed a lot of school and was known as "the girl with asthma," the one with whom you had to be careful.

My mother was not one to coddle; when I stayed home from school, she set me up in front of the television with a cup of hot chocolate and a blanket, and that was that. I always felt that my mother disapproved of sickness and that she never quite believed I was as sick as I claimed.

My father would inevitably come home from work and tease me: "Malingering, *again?*"

I always felt guilty for being sick, felt that I was somehow indulging in an unacceptable weakness, felt that I should be able to tough out anything my body gave me.

So here I am with the deadliest disease of our time, and I receive a profusion of sympathy; I will never be called a malingerer again. Today everyone knows I am legitimately ill, and responds accordingly. Instead of soaking up the attention, however, I shun it, smooth over the pains and the infections, try to tough it out although nobody except myself tells me I have to.

I cannot shake the feeling that if I admit I am dying, I will indeed begin to die. There is one thing I can admit, however.

I am sick of being "the girl with AIDS."

I've often wondered how Bill dodged so many close calls for so many years, how he sank to the depths of the most insidious, debilitating infections only to rise to the heights of living despite them. How, for all intents and purposes, he gave the finger to death time after time.

Henry summed it up perfectly. "You're hot stuff," he said, "in more ways than one," when Bill roasted with a 105-degree fever but still remembered to thank Henry for treating him.

Bill was also downright stubborn. He'd be damned if he'd let something like a fever make him impolite.

Bill learned his lessons well; his intellect and wit allowed him to master the murkiest geometric proof, remember every rule of grammar so that his speech as well as his writing never contained a single dangling participle.

In fact, there was never anything I thought Bill couldn't master, except possibly dancing, which he abhorred for good reason. He had no natural sense of rhythm and never found

*any release in surrendering to music. Dancing represented
Bill's ultimate fear: to lose control and be viewed by others
as disordered. To be viewed as, heaven forbid, goofy.*

Perfection and self-control ruled Bill's life. He walked like
a well-trained soldier, back as straight as steel, shoulders
never hunched. Always meticulously groomed, his hair was
legendary, and a source of pride to Bill. One of the ways Bill
relaxed, if he ever really did relax, was to put on a sweat suit
and run a hand through his hair so that it stood up like a
thick pompadour, untamed. He never let anyone except me
see him in such a state, but I took a picture once and occasionally blackmailed him with it. He liked my hair best when
it was super-short and very neat, very predictable, no
cowlicks marring my surface.

He was hot stuff. He was as eccentric as an eighty-year-
old by the time I met him at eighteen. He was so damned mature, so serious, that you couldn't help but laugh. And Bill
saw his own eccentricity and laughed right along.

Bill had a beautiful voice, deep and resonant; a reporter
once asked if he had ever considered a radio career. Having
known Bill, I must wonder if he cultivated his voice as one of
the few physical things, like his hair, that he could control. I
have to believe he did. He was a wonderful public speaker; I
never once heard him stutter. In fact, I don't remember ever
hearing him say "Um . . ." when asked a question in any
context. Bill always had an opinion and was always happy to
share it.

He often gave presentations at work because he was so
skilled at simplifying difficult concepts. He particularly loved
using props: slide projectors, multimedia computer systems,
charts and graphs. My family traditionally plays board
games after Thanksgiving dinner, boys against girls. One
year we were playing Trivial Pursuit when a question arose
as to whether the girls had moved their token a few extra
spaces. In the middle of good-natured banter, Bill whipped

out a pointer from his shirt pocket, extended it, and tapped it on the board, counting, "One, two, three . . ." as we all dissolved in laughter.

I never did find out why he had that pointer with him in the first place.

This was Bill. He never took himself too seriously.

Which was a good thing, because he really was silly at times. Many of his silly moments came with my sister Dolores. She once found a bat flying around her apartment and called Bill for help. No fan of bats himself, Bill nonetheless bravely went over. The bat swooped while my sister and niece screamed. Bill looked around for a weapon and found a can of air freshener. He sprayed it at the bat, who only staggered a little before flying away, smelling quite lovely. Bill then spotted a racquetball racquet and brandished it like a sword. He was not an athlete, but he did know how to play tennis. He used his serve to bat that bat toward the window. He didn't try to kill it—Bill didn't like to harm anything, no matter how loathsome—but he kept at it until—SCORE!—he found an opening and the bat sailed out of the apartment.

There are other moments: an outing at a roller rink where everyone skated in one direction while Dolores and Bill unintentionally skated in the other, crashing into walls and fellow skaters. Another: Dolores and Bill on a New England ski slope, falling down the bunny trail, falling off the T-bar, trying to hold each other up, but laughing so hard they couldn't. Giving up and tumbling into the lounge, never to reemerge on the mountain.

Bill was the type of person who would hear an idea once and, no matter how casually introduced, think he had to follow through on it immediately. I learned this early in our relationship. All I had to do was say something like "Gee, aren't those little laptop computers nice?" and the next day one would appear. This made casual conversation dangerous, because Bill always took every suggestion as his march-

ing orders, and he marched. I think this is probably why we went on so many vacations and had such nice homes. Bill took me very seriously and got right on everything I said.

Bill also habitually stockpiled possessions, although most of our homes weren't big enough to accommodate them: a case of paper towels, cartons of ballpoint pens, three tool-boxes crammed full of wrenches in every conceivable size. I once opened his dresser drawer and gazed at the clothing stuffed inside: sixty pairs of socks, thirty-five pairs of underwear in assorted sizes, all bought so that Bill would be prepared should his weight change suddenly. Bill liked to think he could avert whatever disaster might strike. He liked to think nothing could get the best of him.

Bill never thought AIDS would actually kill him. It would give him a run for his money, certainly, but I think he found that exhilarating in a way, his ultimate challenge. Although he was a learned man, perhaps he didn't know enough to die.

I thank God Bill was ignorant for so long.

I sometimes think the greatest thing AIDS did for Bill was teach him humility. At the end he finally learned the lesson he had resisted for almost eight years. And the lesson was this: that he was human. And that, no matter how intelligent, no matter how funny, no matter how wonderful and how courageous and how tenacious, humans remain humans.

And humans die.

PART SIX: 1992

I recently started building a dollhouse. I cut; I glue; I sand smooth the edges of life in one-inch scale. I control this fabricated world; every molding and stair tread is conceived by me and born of my hands.

No surprises lurk below the surface of this contrived Victorian. And no figures reside in my dollhouse. The absence of life within its walls precludes any possibility of death.

In this world, I don't have AIDS.

New Year

New years can be a lot like old years, and this year is no exception.

Once again I am in my accustomed position at the hospital, looking downriver, looking at the parking lot, looking through ripped window screens littered with the bodies of the bugs no medicine could save. Looking, a passenger on a ship inside a bottle, at potential life, but unable to squeeze through the neck to live it.

I am now formally disabled and will collect a fixed income, and dust, for at least another five years, when I will be reevaluated to determine if I died in the interim.

Henry says I am not in the terminal stage of illness; after much internal debate, I have decided that this is good. My vital organs are still intact, valiantly fighting my infections and the deleterious effects of medications, thus leaving me in an uneasy state of nondeterioration and nonimprovement.

My skin, the organ that holds me together, is crumbling, peeling like the skin of rotting fruit, exposing its soft middle. I will soon be nothing but plump, breathing innards and a stubborn brain, a creature worthy of H. G. Wells, literally stripped to the bone.

I am on a sedative now, ostensibly to control the nausea that causes me to stop every ten minutes to sit, breathe, and heave. Because I am quietly sedated, each movement is protracted, and whole conversations and hours spent in this hospital are forgotten whispers. I feel like the main character in Charlotte Perkins Gilman's novel *The Yellow Wallpaper:* Confined to bed by male authorities for so long, the heroine crawls in circles around her room, shoulder pressed to the wall, and struggles to enter the pattern of its wallpaper.

I fantasize about receiving a gift certificate for one day without AIDS, but even in my dreams I cannot redeem it. I once convinced myself I would make Henry famous by being the first person to be cured of this disease, but I've stopped dreaming of miracles, reluctantly acknowledging that Henry's fame, as far as I'm concerned, may have to come through an obscure discovery made at autopsy.

But this is not the worst thing that could happen, after all. Perhaps it is the Ativan, or perhaps it is the hypnotic drip of IV fluids that keeps away the panic, makes posthumous recognition somehow acceptable. Perhaps it is the Ativan, perhaps it is simply the passing of time, but today I feel little regret.

Today when I touch the crucifix hanging on a gold chain around my neck, I understand.

Engulfed

Dream: July 1, 1992

I am in an American small town during World War II, an industrial town with concrete buildings and cracked sidewalks. I stand in front of a wooden structure the size of a small room. It has four entrances and is made from oversized Lincoln Logs. Inside, people lie stacked on their backs; they are packed in as tightly as slaves were packed on ships. The people inside do not struggle. Their hands are tied.

I carry a long wooden match, the kind used to light fireplaces. Without any remorse, I strike it and touch the building; the structure goes up in flames. Although I hear no screams, I know I have just committed murder. Someone else strikes another match, and soon the entire building is engulfed in flames. Outside, a man runs away from pursuers in orange and gray uniforms, men who are young and blond and well built. The man falls to his stomach and crawls into the burning structure. I realize it is Bill's former hospital roommate, a man who died several years ago from AIDS. I laugh and tell him he doesn't want to go in there. But I don't help him; I don't even watch to see what happens to him.

I was only following orders, I think.

Flash to a different place in the same town, to a room dark and gutted. Lying on a bed is a young fair-haired man. He is quite thin and has blood on his arm. An officer orders me to care for him, and another woman, a nurse, soon joins me. But I don't let her near him; I want to take care of him myself.

The patient is friendly and allows me to dress his wounds. But just when I think I'm done, he rolls over and I see blood on his back. I clean him again, only to discover that his other arm now bleeds.

I ask what happened.

He laughs bitterly and says, "We knew all about it in the 1990s, but we didn't change anything."

I know he will not live much longer.

I leave the room, only to realize that the uniformed men are now chasing me. I duck into an official-looking building. My heart pounds as I run up and down countless stairways in search of an exit. I finally reach a safe area; I open a door and see a fountain bathed in light. It reminds me of a museum; it is very peaceful. I approach a small group of young gay men. They have no visible marks or injuries. They smile when they see me, and say I must take an elevator with them if I ever hope to escape.

I feel as if I belong with them, and step into the elevator. The doors close behind us, and I wake up.

Divine Insight

It was sometime between the moment the nurse's aide came into my hospital room with my lunch and the point at which I unwrapped my mixed raw vegetable salad with French dressing that the simplest and most amazing thought came to me:

I trust in God.

Thoughts forever swim through my head, but they are usually of a more mundane variety. For example, in a given day I may have two dozen intimate conversations with myself in which I never actually open my mouth. These conversations often consist of witty retorts I should have made, of the things I would have said had I reacted more quickly. In most cases, these scenes place me in the best possible light, which rarely happens in reality.

I spend much of my quiet and inactive time rehearsing for my active and noisy periods. In some cultures and in some eras, our own not excluded, I would have been accused of hearing voices. I would have been confined to a room in a concrete building, a room containing only a bed and a water pitcher.

Is this so far removed from where I've ended up after all?

But why this sudden burst of divine insight when my previous thoughts that day were largely confined to whether I would be able to pee in a jar on demand? Perhaps the absurdity of life in general, and the absurdity of my life in particular, finally revealed itself at the sight of another tray bearing plastic cutlery and straws with bendy middles. Perhaps I was left with no other choice but to accept that these are not the core pieces of life but merely some of its more bizarre accoutrements.

Maybe the "why" doesn't really matter that much. If some people can be reborn by falling down in a church aisle or stepping into a bath at Lourdes, why can't I be spiritually rekindled in a beige hospital room in Yonkers, hooked to an IV, a television speaker propped against my head because the medicines I have taken to save my life have made me near-deaf?

And if I'm not like Lazarus, and will not miraculously rise from this bed, then so what? I will still have my internal conversations, which are my own precious gifts to myself.

Angry Musical

The theatergoers buzzed noisily, flitting in their undersized seats, studying their programs so they would know exactly which number came when, negotiating seat-arm proprieties with their neighbors. With the first few notes of the overture came an anticipatory quiet; forgotten were the problems of where to put the coats and how to see around the person in the row ahead.

The show was called *Falsettos*. We were eager to see it because AIDS was its central theme. But with the first notes, soaring and dissipating to pinnacles and depths all around me, energetically dancing into every crevice and crack of the vaulted ceiling, I realized I had wasted my money on a show about AIDS. Because AIDS had taken my hearing away and, with it, my ability to turn cacophony into harmony, discord into an experience so intense you must hold your breath until the notes fade, until you must exhale and think: Of course. It had to happen like this.

I took piano lessons for twelve years, assuming from the first moment I played a one-handed melody that music would be mine for the rest of my life. I still remember that moment. I was watching my sister play the piano one afternoon when I was about seven years old. This was the sister closest to me in age, the one whose stomach I once bit in a fury. The perpetrator of a notorious family crime: a couple of years earlier, she had wrapped the overhead light cord around my neck and pushed me off the bed, undoubtedly hoping to be done with me once and for all. "It will be like you're riding a swing," she said, and of course I agreed to it, being only five at the time. I swung for only a second; the entire fixture came loose from the ceiling, and I suffered nothing more than a bruised ego for having been so gullible. This is the same sister whose feet I used to swaddle in blankets and call "the twins," coddling them like dolls, creating conversations and worlds in which they starred.

As I watched her play "The First Noel," two thoughts crossed my mind. The first was: Why does she get to do this and I don't? The second was: I can do that.

I watched, mesmerized, until finally she left and I put my right hand down where her right hand had been, and played e-d-c-d-e-f-g. There it was, my first Christmas carol. I asked my mother that day if I could begin lessons.

Of course my sister was older and far more skilled, which made me more determined to practice. For a while we both took lessons from Sister Immaculata, who had a mean heart, or so it seemed to me as a child. A woman who hysterically chirped, "Don't look at the keys when you play!" and covered our shaking hands with a heavy book. In olden days a ruler across the knuckles would have driven home her point, but this was the seventies and such punishment was unacceptable. Nevertheless, I quickly learned to move my hands instinctively over the keyboard, feeling where they should land rather than seeing them touch down, a skill I still use today at my computer.

My sister eventually stopped taking lessons. To me, the song "To Each His Dulcinea" from *Man of La Mancha* will forever be hers; she memorized it and played it flawlessly. But I was never completely happy with the way she played; it sounded packaged, mechanical, to me. I know now it was her halfheartedness that bothered me; her music did not have the soul to make it come alive.

Years later, while I was preparing my repertoire for college, my piano teacher said, "It's not enough to get the notes right; you have to put yourself in the composer's place and feel what he felt." From that moment I pictured myself an eccentric old man when I played the music of Papa Haydn, or a brilliant court composer when playing Mozart. I constructed a story to go with every movement I played; the fast trill sequence in Chopin's "Grande Valse Brilliante" became someone falling down the stairs, head over foot. A slower section was the murmur of lovers walking under the moon on a sultry night.

In the end, passion conquered technique. Although often praised for a lovely touch, I was as often chastised for trying to hide blatantly incorrect notes with rounded, emotional tones. I was unable to play both accurately and beautifully, so I gave up my professional dreams and decided to allow music to remain my love, if not my vocation.

Music was so integral to my identity that it became my distinguishing feature.

"You know her, she's the piano player," people said.

I became the accompanist for a number of school and church choruses at an early age. Several times I had the opportunity to play on the huge church organ in the choir loft, high above the congregation. Terror struck when I first gazed upon the two keyboards for my hands and the Brobdingnagian keyboard for my feet. Unless I split into four pieces, I thought, I'll never be able to produce a pleasurable piece of music on this instrument.

I made so many mistakes at first that I gave up on the pedals altogether. But eventually, as with so many experiences in life, time and success bolstered my confidence and I gingerly pressed my feet to the pedals. "Faith of Our Fathers" trumpeted forth in organistic glory. Suddenly my whole body was part of the music, fingers and feet moving independently and yet so dependently, proclaiming an exhilarating, amazing, transcendent song.

I associate every period of my life with music. Childhood lived within the score of *My Fair Lady;* adolescence had moments as contradictory as "Clair de Lune" and "Born to Run." The first song of my married life was "The Rose" by Bette Midler; its opening measures, the steady repetition of a single chord, take me back to that day when Bill and I saw in each other a lifetime filled with a hundred fertile possibilities.

I cannot think of things happy or sad without also calling to mind some measure of music; in effect, each scene of my life has its own unique score. Even as I write these words, a twenty-nine-year-old woman who feels her body succumb to the power that is AIDS, the music of *Les Miserables* comes to mind, words and music that speak of lost dreams and the price of love.

In my family, singing with or without the radio was acceptable, even expected. Every morning my mother turned on WNEW-AM and sang to the big band sound of Tommy Dorsey. Car rides were always very musical; my parents sang to whatever was on the radio, and my sister and I sang to whatever was in our heads at the time—rarely the same melody. I went into marriage thinking that everyone sang out loud and spontaneously, that humming while brushing your teeth was normal. Ironically, I married a man with a tin ear.

I've never heard music played in his parents' house just for the pleasure of it; I have never heard their voices raised in song. I find this lack of music strange, sad.

But today Bill experienced the catharsis of music, while now I sit on a homeward-bound train, eyes brimming, not knowing if I cry because of what I visually discerned or what, musically, I could not.

I was angry during that musical, so angry I almost ripped the hearing aids from my ears and threw them over the balcony. The only thing that stopped me was the thought of the money wasted; we had just finished paying off the hearing aids' $1,300 price tag. Thirteen hundred dollars is a lot of money; it is the cost of a two-month supply of AZT. This is how I think after living with HIV for so many years: the value of money is only as great as its ability to buy medicine. It was the thought of the wasted money that kept the hearing aids in my ears, the thought that I might, in effect, toss away money that could have been used to extend a life.

The headphones provided by the theater probably worked for most people who needed them that night, those who were mildly deaf, or naturally hard of hearing because of advanced age. They were useless to me. The insides of my ears are bruised and sore from violently pressing the earpieces into them in a desperate attempt to understand even one line of a song. My ears now throb, not from having heard too much, too loudly, but from not having heard anything at all.

I am angry because my music is gone; it has been scooped from the heart of me as casually as I would scoop the pulp from a pumpkin. The loss of music in my life hurts more than neuropathy or nodules. My musical edge is gone, and I feel like the kid in my school whose voice was such a hopelessly untuned instrument that he was told not to sing during the class show.

I lost my hearing gradually. It started as a gentle buzz, a ring so pianissimo as to be almost undetectable. But then it grew more insistent; every drop of Amikacin, every shot of streptomycin, given with the hope of destroying the bacteria that was destroying me, cranked up the internal volume a little higher until finally the noise inside became greater, more prevalent, than the noise outside. Every time I connected the bag of medicine to the catheter surgically implanted in my chest for this purpose I made an irreversible choice: my hearing for my life. Of course I chose life; perfect hearing is useless when you're dead. But had I anticipated the deadening influence of deafness, the introduction of a certain joylessness that had never existed before, I might well have chosen to disconnect myself from my bottle of life a little sooner.

Music, once soothing, now annoys me; high notes and low notes are homogenized into a single off-key whine. The only music I enjoy now is old music, music from the past, music that still lives in my head, in a place where my brain and my memories fill in the gaps left by my ears.

Think of the wail of a modem when it connects. This is what I hear now instead of words or song. Think of the constant drone of the subways, the almost electric murmur on the platforms even when the train is absent; think of the sound of a hundred bees in a hive. These are the melodies I hear. Think of what it would be like to have your ear pressed constantly to a seashell, to have all sound engulfed by the persistence of nature, by the constant swish-crash of the waves. This is what I hear.

But it is what I do not hear that grieves me most. At night I am virtually deaf, entombed in a crypt of darkness and silence. I sleep touching Bill at all times; since I cannot hear him breathe, I must feel him breathe to reassure myself that he does indeed breathe. He does things in the darkness that I know nothing about; once, for example, he vomited in bed, and I didn't wake up. He tells me he often leaves our room in the middle of the night and returns hours later, and I don't even stir.

I am afraid that one morning I will wake up and find he has died in his sleep, that he called for me one last time, and that I did not hear.

These are the fears of the near-deaf; these are the fears that permeate a world where meanings are almost fathomed and reactions almost made. They are the songs that are sung without words; they are the songs that are sung without music.

Some people think guardian angels have wings.

I know better.

They have stethoscopes.

I first met Henry—or as I called him then, Dr. Frey—in March 1987. Bill had been diagnosed a few weeks earlier and was now under Henry's care. I made an appointment to have my own blood tested by him on a Wednesday evening.

During those early days, Bill and I often went to see Henry separately, not yet needing to know every detail of each other's cells, blindly trusting that things could not change that much from visit to visit. So on that night in 1987 I went alone to be tested and didn't think it strange that I did. I'm sure I sat for hours in the waiting room, and I'm sure I was irritated at having to wait. It was too soon for me to understand just how many people had AIDS and just how much care each of them required.

Henry's secretary, Lydia, ushered me into the back exami-nation room, joking that Henry was nicknamed "Dr. Drac-

ula" because of the amount of blood he drew. Her insight
didn't comfort me; I already had a history of fainting around
needles. Still, I had no choice but to sit and wait and worry.
Lydia gave me a paper gown; this was the first and only time
I ever wore one there. After the first visit, we dispensed with
such formalities, and now I just take off whatever needs to be
taken off when it needs to be taken off, without the least bit of
embarrassment.

Henry came in with his head down, reading my chart. But
I immediately sensed that he studied me out of the corner of
his eye, that he quickly paired me with the twenty-two-year-
old man he had recently met. I subsequently learned that
Henry angled the vertical blinds in his office in such a way
that he could sit at his desk and invisibly observe his patients
as they approached. I don't know how many times he has
said to me, "I watched you walk up the path tonight. You're
fine." And I always am.

Over the years I have learned that Henry rarely misses a
thing.

When Henry finally looked up and shook my hand, I
thought: Oh, Bill, you've done it again. Bill was never one to
drown in adjectives, and so I had extrapolated my own picture of Henry from Bill's vague description. I expected to
meet a chubby man in his sixties who talked nonstop and
used a lot of big words. Instead, I shook hands with a handsome man in his early forties with amazing blue eyes. And,
although it was well controlled on that first visit, Henry's
good humor immediately revealed itself. He did use big
words, most of which were incomprehensible to me, but I realized he didn't use them to show off; he used them because
they expressed most succinctly what he needed to say.

Henry was not at all what I expected, and I knew this was
a good thing.

Henry then took my blood; we made an appointment to go
over the results. But the thought of having to wait weeks and

weeks for the news, good or bad, made me anxious. I asked if we could dispense with formalities, if Henry could give me the required counseling over the phone when my results came back. He saw my anxiety and agreed to make an exception.

I never had a chance to call. Henry called me at work and said, "Go somewhere where you can talk privately." I locked myself in an empty office. There I heard the words I had dreaded and denied: "Your test came back positive."

We probably spoke for forty-five minutes. I'm sure my boss wondered where I'd gone, but I didn't care. Henry gave me more attention on the phone that day than I suspect many doctors give their patients in a lifetime of office visits.

That phone call established my trust in Henry; I trusted that he had my best interests at heart. I have never stopped trusting him; he has given me years and years of assiduous loving care.

During this first phone call Henry launched into one of his now-famous lectures on the medical aspects of HIV, trying for all the world to put a rational, scientific framework around something so emotionally devastating.

With his help we have been able to live as normal a life as possible, even when normalcy seems like something meant only for other people. His words became our gospel.

There are people who hit their knees to pray, who clack beads or light candles and call it prayer. There are people who equate the truth with words and icons and call it faith. And then there are the truly devout, the people who cherish the beauty of bile and saliva and bacteria and sweat, who look for miracles in spilled blood, find meaning in the trusting faces of their patients. These are the people who live their religion.

These are the people whose lives we should feast.

As time passed and AIDS asserted itself more aggressively into our lives, so did Henry. Soon Bill and I talked about our disease so often that it became too cumbersome to say "Dr. Frey" in our everyday conversations. To each other, then, he simply became Henry.

After a while, I ventured to call Henry by his first name when I saw him, to move our relationship to a different level through a reduction in words, and he allowed my hesitant familiarity.

Henry readily says "I don't know" when he doesn't know, and doesn't worry about his reputation when he says it. He said this to me many times during 1991, when I first experienced the invasive nodular process later identified as M. haemophilum *infection.*

"I don't know what this is," he said when first one, then two, then three nodules appeared.

"I don't know what's going on," he said when erupting lesions appeared on my face and ear.

"I don't know," he said when I pleaded with him to reveal what treatment would save me.

Like a bird of prey, he hovered around this mycobacterium in ever-closing circles. He did every conceivable test, consulted with anyone who could possibly help. He never gave up.

After almost a year of saying "I don't know," Henry came into my hospital room one morning.

"I know what you have," he said.

He then started me on the treatment that has prolonged my life beyond everyone's expectations. All because Henry was willing to admit from the start that he didn't know, and was willing to do whatever was necessary to change that fact.

During one of my early hospitalizations, I was admitted to a private room that happened to be on the pediatric ward. The nurses there craved adult conversation and gave me juice and cookies every night; it was nice to be coddled. One afternoon Henry had to do a particularly painful surgi-

cal excision on my right thigh. Doused in Demerol I slipped in and out of sleep for the rest of the day.

At eleven that night I received my last dose of painkiller and drifted off. At about midnight I awoke with the feeling of being watched. In the dark, in a chair by my bed, sat Henry, just looking, perhaps hoping that the cover of night would reveal to him what daytime tests could not.

"I don't think I'll be able to stay awake," I whispered. "The Demerol . . ."

"Don't worry about staying awake for me," he said, and I didn't, falling instead into a comfortable, peaceful rest. Knowing, through one man's midnight ministrations, that when it came time for me to die, I would not die alone.

Henry is an old-fashioned doctor in a world where dividing a patient into treatable segments dominates, where a doctor is always supposed to remain at arm's length. Instead, Henry rolls up his sleeves and plunges ahead without fearing the consequences of caring. During Bill's most serious illness, Henry said, "I have to work very hard to separate my emotions from my medicine." He managed to treat Bill in the medically responsible manner, although he was already emotionally involved. He struggled, yet succeeded in keeping that involvement from compromising his work.

The relationship Bill and I developed with Henry may be unique in the universe of doctor-patient relationships, but it is certainly not unique in Henry's world. All of his patients react the same way when asked their opinion of him. We all shake our heads and call him a character. We smile. We can't believe how lucky we are. His office is plastered with pictures and presents and postcards; his goodness and devotion are the therapy to which his beloved patients cling.

Throughout Bill's suffering, Henry was there, holding his hand in the operating room, giving instructions over the phone if he couldn't be there physically. When Bill lost his blood pressure on a Sunday night, the nurses miraculously reached Henry before he went out for a jog. He entered Bill's room minutes later wearing sneakers, shorts, a stethoscope, and a T-shirt reading "No pain, no gain." In this ludicrous outfit he revived Bill and saved his life. I've lost count of how many times Henry intervened at just the right moment, how many times he bought us just a little more time. He kept doing this for Bill until he no longer could, until saving him would have become more cruel than losing him.

Henry understood from the beginning that sick people have the same needs and dreams as the well. He saw my turmoil and treated my "but what if?" questions with respect.

"I want you to know I would personally raise any child you might have," he said at a time when childlessness seemed unbearable to me. This is the kind of man he is.

As the years passed, Bill and I became good friends with Henry; we thought of ourselves as the Three Musketeers. We went to each other's homes; we exchanged presents at holidays. One of my hospitalizations ended on my twentyninth birthday. When Henry arrived to do my discharge exam, my mind was on a million things: seeing Bill again, kissing my puppy, getting home. Henry had me sit on the bed, first in one place, then another, then another. Finally, exasperated, he said I'd make a lousy princess because I couldn't feel what was under my mattress. A birthday present lay hidden under the covers; in my excitement to be gone, I hadn't even noticed.

For Henry there is little separation between his personal life and his work, and this suits him. He once said that he has a hussy and her name is medicine. He donates his blood and his platelets to his patients; he donates his services to a Haitian hospital when it is short-staffed in the summer. He gives his strength to those who need it. He once waited for my friend at the emergency room; he carried her into the hospital himself when she finally arrived.

There's a lot of talk about angels these days: books on the best-seller lists, television exposés, and so forth. These angels are always supernatural and ethereal and magical. But I think there are angels among us who are substantial and tangible and real.

I like to live my love stories on earth; I don't like thinking that love exists only in the clouds or in a future place.

I like to think some angels have amazing blue eyes.

PART SEVEN: 1993

The song "Amazing Grace" was sung at Alice's funeral. You know the words.

In our politically correct times, the word "wretch" had been changed to "soul."

Afterward Bill said, "We're in trouble if we start believing we're not wretched."

PART SEVEN: 1993

Circular Thoughts

January 27, 1993 ——————————————

We stand in line with hundreds of others at Universal Studios and wait almost an hour to board the ride touted as the best in Orlando, and which lasts a full five minutes.

Like the Minotaur, we are trapped within an intricate maze. We wind our way around hospital green dividers and think that every turn will show us a way out; we travel a very short distance in a very protracted fashion. These lines keep us constantly moving and anticipating, but also keep us from clearly seeing our destination. And ultimately, the destination never quite lives up to its promise.

A cynic might compare this to sex: a grand buildup, some dodging and weaving, the deed done almost before it started. But I don't think I'm that cynical; even when I played the romance game years ago, I was too naive to be jaded.

I think I'll stretch this analogy to absurd lengths: a theme park line is like the long haul of AIDS.

Each new medicine, each remission promises a happy ending yet unseen.

Each relapse, each opportunistic infection, portends an unhappy ending yet unseen.

In either case we inch forward and anticipate both the best and the worst, satisfied to just prolong the journey itself.

Senselessness

What will I do if I develop CMV retinitis and go blind, go blind when I'm already half deaf?

I would be left barely alive.

Or left too much alive.

AIDS has uncovered my terror, my deepest fears. I am a musical person, a person often called a good listener. I depended on sound so much that I could never imagine living without it. Becoming deaf was incomprehensible to me.

This is what happened.

Although I retain enough hearing to function, I no longer trust that I will even keep what I now have. The next outbreak of *M. haemophilum* may require using more ototoxic drugs just to save my life. I could easily lose the little hearing that remains.

As it is, I now often read lips. My eyes translate the words that my ears no longer hear.

Many HIV-infected people develop CMV retinitis; some of these people go blind. I have lived the terror of losing my hearing; I may also live the terror of losing my vision. I have heard of children born blind and deaf, of children who lose their senses early and find a way to compensate for this loss and discover a way to live that still resembles human living.

I am too old to compensate for the loss of two senses.

I think it would be easier to live sensory-deprived if you had never known what it was like to have the senses. I fear I will become like a one-cell organism, capable of basic functioning but little else.

This is my new terror. I'm afraid this will happen.

I've decided, as much as one can decide such a thing, that I will kill myself should this scenario play out. But how? I don't have a stockpile of Seconal to do the trick. But even if I did, would I necessarily die? I've survived more than my share already; I might dodge the odds again and make myself into the vegetative organism I fear.

Then there are the logistics of suicide. I wouldn't want Bill to find me; that would be much too gruesome. So I would have to go outside, to a park, perhaps, and hope the police would find me before a stray dog.

(I knew a guy with AIDS who once considered blowing out his brains in a forest. He decided against it, however, because he feared his blood would harm the animals who lived there.)

I hope these thoughts remain simply words on paper. Death does not frighten me so much as the thought of living entombed in darkness and silence, of living as a blob of uncontrollable excretions and incoherent mumblings.

Of living senselessly.

Choices

Dream: February 9, 1993 _____

Bill is in the army during the Vietnam War. While I wait faithfully for his return to the States, I receive a telegram informing me that Bill and a buddy have been arrested for attempted rape. I flash to a scene in which he and his friend swing a silver club near a bathing woman.

I fly to the army base, but he won't talk to me when I arrive. Although the charges are eventually dropped, I suspect a cover-up. I investigate on my own and learn not only that the victim is a prostitute but that there is an unusual, undefined relationship between Bill and his buddy.

I enlist in the army, although Bill still refuses my company; he is distant, arrogant, patronizing. Hurt, I cry, "You must talk to me! I've invested all this time and travel in you!"

I suddenly notice my shoes, dung-colored sandals with thick rubber heels: elderly, nunlike. I realize I am wasting my youth here, and I exchange my sandals and khaki uniform for black stiletto heels and tight blue jeans. I leave my commitment to the army and to Bill behind.

I don't get very far. A hand-lettered sign advertises my services for sixty dollars an hour; I am now a prostitute serving the base. Bill's commanding officer, who looks suspiciously like Norman Schwarzkopf, hires me and brings Bill along. Clearly, Bill is uncomfortable. I prepare them both a nice dinner served in an old-fashioned kitchen, and the mere homeliness of the meal pleases the officer.

However, I wasn't hired for my culinary skills, and Bill is ordered to remain in the room for the duration of what apparently will follow. The officer kisses me, and Bill doubles over, sobbing. He touches my abdomen and begs, "Please don't do anything down here!" The commanding officer smiles and leaves, and I realize he contrived the situation to reunite us.

As we hug, Bill murmurs into my shoulder, "What have I made you do?"

I reply, "What I have done is my own choice."

Bill: A Short Story

October 18, 1993 _____

It is not the first time this has happened, this midnight disruption, this unrelenting chorus of "you must write about Bill" pounding incessantly, pinning me in place like a mother at a grade school play whose child doesn't appear until the last act.

I have not written much about Bill.

Everything I have written is about Bill.

I know I can write about him. At least I know I can write anecdotes that will reveal his nature to some degree. But to commit Bill to paper, to neatly package his life, wrap it up in crisp brown paper and tie it closed with string, this feels too much like reading the ending before knowing the plot. I don't want to reach the end of his book; I'm afraid my very words will place boundaries around a life that should be boundless.

But the chorus will continue unless I write about Bill.

I will begin the story two months ago, when other concerns kept me awake.

It is two-thirty in the morning, and Bill sleeps on his side, knees together. When I lie like that, my thighs sigh into each other and form a wide, solid mass. But when I look at Bill, I see the beams from the streetlamp through the inch of space that separates his legs.

God, he's getting thin, I think.

Only six months ago Bill was twenty pounds overweight; liver and heart problems made him retain water like a camel. Well-meaning people chided him about eating too well, not knowing he spent a good portion of each day losing the little he managed to swallow.

He's been thin since I met him. He was eighteen then, lean as only young, hungry men can be lean. Leanness must be natural to him; in the ten-plus years I've known him, I have never once seen him exercise intentionally. He was built, as Henry later commented, like a swimmer or a wrestler—broad on top with sturdy, substantial legs. Except for eyeglasses and one single silver hair, he has not changed much.

He was once mistaken for my younger brother, but that was many years ago. His face and outlook have long since surrendered their innocence.

He has aged well.

From pictures, I know he was a beautiful baby, with big, alert eyes and a fine round head, "like a caesarean baby's," the obstetrician said. One evening earlier this year his mother and I sat up late, passing the time until we could once again visit Bill in the hospital. She tamped out her cigarette and immediately lit another; her eyes filled, and she looked toward some place far away from this lonely apartment in Yonkers, to a place where her oldest son did not have AIDS.

"He didn't like to move around a lot," she said. "He was like a baby Buddha, content to sit and observe."

Although his younger sister repeatedly surpassed him in physical feats—walking at a younger age, riding a two-wheeler months earlier—he was unintimidated. Bill said he always knew that what he lacked in brawn he made up for in brains. Even today he does not fight his disease by embracing exercise programs or snake oil treatments. He fights his disease by learning everything he can about it and then trying to outwit it.

He had a brief sports career as a child. He joined a Little League team for two seasons because his best friend was a member. Relegated to right field, Bill was less than spectacular. He umped for a while, but stopped after he made a controversial call and was harassed. ("I *know* that was a strike," he recently said.) He gave up on sports altogether when his doctor discovered a problem with the mitral valve of his heart. He never took a gym class after the sixth grade as a result.

He's not a total washout physically. He's a decent tennis player, although we don't play together because I play so poorly. And he has tremendous stamina, stamina that has served him well. Today, when I urge him to exercise to keep his body as strong as possible for as long as possible, he smiles at me from his computer and wiggles his fingers, and says that typing gives him quite a workout.

He was always the smart one, the brilliant one, the straight-A student. He was a Cub Scout and a Boy Scout, a paperboy and an altar boy. Valedictorian of his eighth grade class, he stood on a box behind the lectern and trumpeted, "And on this rock I will build my church, and the gates of hell shall not prevail against it!"

He had a crush on a neighborhood girl, whose dark Italian looks were worlds away from the red-haired Irish girl he married. Once, he rode his bike around and around in front of her house, hoping to see her, and crashed headfirst into a parked car. This is an early example of the compelling—and sometimes disastrous—quality of Bill's love.

He remembers himself as a typical suburban kid. The oldest of three children, he was, and is, the dependable and responsible one, the person to call when a problem needs solving. Relatives tell me that even as a child his confidence and vocabulary were the envy of adults.

I feel as if I am writing my husband's eulogy, desperately putting pieces of him on paper so he will be remembered as a good and decent person and not as an AIDS caricature. As a boy who had crushes, a boy who wore a little green scout uniform decorated with merit badges, a boy who lived next door and cut your lawn and shoveled your driveway. A boy who grew up and dangled his foot in the water's edge of adulthood for such a short time, and so gingerly, only to be swept away in the tidal wave of AIDS.

When Bill was twelve years old, he was brutally raped on four or five different occasions by an older boy. This is all I know. I was the first person he told about this experience, years after it occurred. In a 1985 letter to me, Bill wrote: "There is really nothing else that can be said about that. . . . I began to hate him and really never spoke to him again. Of course, I didn't tell anyone because I had no idea what had happened even though I knew it shouldn't have happened."

Bill and I went to England as college juniors to conduct research as part of our scholarship program. Bill studied the computer technology available for handicapped children; I explored support networks for victims of sexual violence. Bill repeatedly pressed me to acknowledge the male rape victim when I reported my findings. He knew firsthand that they existed, and he wouldn't let me off the hook.

During one of our training sessions, a fellow student made a joke about inmates being raped in prison.

Bill got up and left the room.

I followed, and found him in tears.

"It's not funny," he said.

Bill later told a psychologist about his experiences, and she drew out some of the details through hypnosis. He has kept these details from me. I think he has kept them from me not out of secrecy or deception but out of a desire that our life together remain untouched by ghosts he thinks exorcised.

I once saw a picture of his attacker in a photo album; Bill pointed to a teenage boy and simply said: "That's him."

When Bill left the room, I tore the picture into a hundred pieces and flushed them down the toilet. I would like to confront this man and hurt him as brutally as he once hurt a little boy. But I never will, because our paths will never cross. I heard he is a husband and father who lives a life seemingly unencumbered by the violence he once inflicted.

Bill applied to and was accepted into some of the most prestigious Catholic high schools in New York. But the tuition at these schools was out of reach of his father's municipal salary. Bill miserably attended public school for exactly six weeks. Then he secretly wrote a letter to the principal of his first high school choice, saying that the school should not only admit him mid-semester but award him a full scholarship as well. His letter prompted a phone call from the principal, and Bill was forced to tell his mother what he had done. Being only thirteen at the time, he needed her to buy him a suit and drive him to the interview.

He was admitted and hired as a woodworker to help offset most of the $3,000-a-year tuition. The staff was undoubtedly amused by this assertive boy who four years later appeared in the yearbook sitting comfortably in a wastepaper basket.

His early success fueled Bill's penchant for letter writing. As a high school freshman, he wrote to the author of his algebra textbook complimenting him on the clarity of his prose. Professionally, his eloquently worded justifications for why he should be promoted and given raise after raise left his bosses with little choice but to comply. Even as I write, letters to the President, the First Lady, the newly appointed AIDS czar, and the editor of the local newspaper wait to be mailed.

Bill's high school years passed rather uneventfully. As part of the speech and debate team, he won an award for reciting Clarence Darrow's closing argument at the Debs trial. He was a four-year member of the Woodworking Club, and his fine carpentry still endures. On the day of his five-year reunion, he took me through his high school and proudly pointed out the new classrooms he had helped construct, the moldings and doors and windows he had framed. He recounted an incident from his woodworking days: once, as he stood on an outside staircase holding a four-by-eight-foot piece of quarter-inch plywood, a huge gust of wind came along and turned the wood into a veritable sail; it lifted Bill up at the top of the stairs and deposited him gently again at the bottom, Mary Poppins–style.

I've probably heard that story fifty times; he tells it whenever the wind kicks up.

Bill won the French Club's Scrabble tournament, and his green plastic "Le Cochon" piggybank trophy still sits on his bureau, although we cut off the snout a few years ago when we needed change for the laundry. He edited the newspaper and the yearbook and graduated in the top five of his high school class. He and his best friend, the former Little Leaguer, collected most of the awards at graduation; Bill went home with the science, English, math, French, and community service honors. He went to the junior prom with a life-long friend and had his first and only girlfriend before me when he was a senior. He considered entering a religious order after graduation—more out of his love for ritual and order than from a deep religious conviction—but his growing confusion about his sexuality caused him to defer this decision.

He often tells me that he'd get a kick out of being the first lay pope.

We are now through Bill's high school years. He was a young man who never got into the least bit of trouble; was, in fact, probably considered a Goody Two-Shoes. He never did drugs, drank beer only a few times at parties, and never got a girl pregnant, broke any hearts, or was arrested. He was polite and neat and conservative and unrebellious. Except for the shadow of violence surrounding his twelfth year, his life had gone more smoothly than anyone had a right to expect.

Nothing should have gone wrong, but it did; the pieces were neatly stacked, but constructed like a house of cards, waiting only for someone to brush against one for all of them to tumble down.

Like many short men, Bill uses his wit to compensate for his lack of physical prowess. His quick mouth, though sometimes too blunt, is more often charming and articulate. He received a full presidential scholarship to Villanova University—room, board, tuition, the works—after meeting with the scholarship committee only once. Although they had many other applicants to consider, the committee members decided Bill's case on the spot. One member later said that his application was so well written that they originally suspected plagiarism.

He always makes a good first impression, always presents his arguments logically and sensibly. These skills allowed him, after college, to quadruple his salary in seven years and persuade his boss to allow him to work at home when his health deteriorated.

Bill finished college in three years. As an undergraduate he immersed himself in the honors program, read calculus to his blind roommate (and occasionally, as a practical joke, rearranged the furniture without his roommate's knowledge), and volunteered almost forty hours a week at a school for severely mentally and physically handicapped children. A man who would gladly sleep until two in the afternoon, Bill nonetheless made it to the children's school for the start of the 6:00 A.M. shift.

Bill loved those kids unconditionally, and they loved him completely in return, running to him when he appeared, clinging to his hand, hugging him around the waist. His job required him to change their diapers and clean up their body fluids; he believes he contracted the hepatitis that now threatens his life during this happy and fulfilling time.

He kept himself so busy during his first year at college that he didn't have time left over to date. Bill and I met at the end of our sophomore year; although we were immediately attracted to each other, Bill was uncharacteristically unassertive in pushing me to ditch my current boyfriend. I kept our relationship on a friendship level, and Bill embarked on the brief relationship that probably infected him.

I've spent countless, sleepless nights thinking, If only I had . . .

During that same summer, the summer of 1983, Bill had an emergency appendectomy. Occasionally he wondered if he received infected blood; at the time, screening blood for HIV was not available. He considered contacting the hospital to settle once and for all the source of his infection, but never made the call. To me, his non-pursuit is a non-apology for his past, for his identity, for what he believes brought him to this point in life. I respect him more for resisting the temptation to possibly metamorphose into what many would term an "innocent" victim of AIDS, someone whose suffering is not perceived to be self-inflicted or deserved.

The source no longer matters; the present remains unchanged.

After graduation, Bill worked for a financial software company, then moved to a major Wall Street firm, and finally returned to his original company. He traveled all over the world on business (he once ended up in the AIDS wing of Westminster Hospital in London); he bought $600 suits from Barney's; his French cuffs were monogrammed. He received his M.B.A., became a registered stockbroker, took classes to become a certified financial planner for people with AIDS, and seemed destined to become his company's youngest vice president. Then, as quickly as a virus invades a cell, it all changed.

Bill became sick, his job was restructured, and he retired at twenty-eight. Now he is an ardent activist. He shoots straight to the top with his concerns; he meets with congressional representatives, writes editorials, and speaks without trepidation. His activism has taken many forms; he is a member of a number of AIDS-related councils and committees and voluntary organizations. He is most effective, however, as a public speaker; he has told his story to thousands of people since 1990. He is particularly impressive when talking to high school students. I think teenagers respect Bill's honesty; I think they appreciate his sincere desire to help them.

This is a thumbnail sketch of Bill's life. It is not enough. It does not show his internal struggles with illness; it does not show the pain he feels when he watches me suffer, or his sadness at not having a son named after him, at not having a daughter named Sarah.

I know he suffers; I know he must suffer, because I do, and we have the same disease. Yet I do not see him cry at night when he thinks I'm asleep. I do not see him grip the table's edge when the reality of his life overwhelms him. I do not see him wallow in pity or regret, take to his bed and escape for a day or a week or a month, as I have been tempted to do.

My descriptions have made him seem barely human, like a clay model of stoicism, but this is not true. He is the best kind of human, the kind who knows his limitations, who knows he cannot control every viral mutation in his world. A human who knows that the best fighter is the one who acknowledges the strength of his opponent, who learns how to successfully duck and weave. Bill lives with an in-your-face attitude toward death. Even though he's disabled, he is busy twenty-four hours a day.

Except when he experiences his major meltdown periods, which occur about every six months. I fear that each one of these episodes will be his last; I've never known anyone who can look quite so wretched when ill.

This past April, Bill embarked on his "great sleep." There is not much to describe: if he was not in motion, he slept. Once, for example, he slept through our nephew's christening party while seated on the living room sofa. After the first hour, the novelty of his behavior wore off and everyone more or less regarded him as an extra cushion. During the "great sleep," he slept profoundly during the night, awoke normally in the morning, ate breakfast, and went back to sleep on the couch, where he remained, barely moving, for the rest of the day.

During this period we decided to buy a condominium in Yonkers, two minutes away from Henry and the hospital. Somehow Bill kept his eyes open long enough to arrange for movers and a mortgage; even at his worst, he is an impeccable organizer. Amid these months of fever and fatigue, he never once neglected to stack his coins neatly from largest to smallest, or to comb his hair with military precision.

The act of moving, to Bill, is a stressor of unknown origin. We've moved three times in the last eight years; within a week after the first two moves, Bill landed in the hospital, once with pneumonia, once with CMV. This year he was hospitalized three weeks before the actual move. He made it to closing, barely, and ruined several checks; I don't know whether sickness or normal closing-day jitters caused their ruin.

Because moving was always so traumatic for Bill, my memories of moving are less than positive. When I think of moving, I inevitably picture myself alone in the new place, deciding it's not as wonderful as I thought. Realizing it's not so wonderful because Bill is not with me.

The "great sleep" lasted until July. It endured just long enough, I remind Bill when he procrastinates over a chore, to ensure his absence during the delights of packing, unpacking, and painting.

Bill's illnesses have a bizarre phantasmagoric quality, especially when fever is involved. He goes into autopilot mode and performs everyday activities without a hitch, deceiving me and everyone else into believing he's fine. The truth is ultimately told when it becomes clear that Bill has absolutely no recollection of his activities, some of which may have been quite extraordinary. For example, he doesn't remember throwing me a surprise birthday party. He doesn't remember throwing up in the employee bathroom of a doughnut shop. He doesn't remember getting a ticket for driving without a seat belt, and he doesn't remember delivering a forty-minute talk on cable television. Yet he did all of these things and will most likely do such things again in a future delirium.

I call these episodes his "fugue states." They are humorous and heartbreaking. Bill is the brightest person I know, and I'm not alone in my opinion; a former client once wrote that she literally considered him a genius. I fool myself into thinking that such a powerful brain must occasionally shut down to recharge, that these occasional blackouts naturally result from a system that is consistently overloaded. How else could I endure listening to him grope for a word, endure seeing his blank look when I refer to something we did together?

How else could I bear to witness these struggles in a man who once considered getting his Ph.D. in higher mathematics because he thought it would be fun?

One of the first signs of illness in Bill is that he becomes a lousy driver. During one fugue state, on the same day he threw me the surprise birthday party, he hit the highway divider twice while driving me home from the hospital. I don't know how we avoided an accident; from some deep part of himself, a part not yet sick, Bill did a quick analysis and recovered his steering. To this day, he will occasionally ask me, "Are you *sure* I hit the divider that day? *Twice?*"

Another time, Bill fell asleep while driving on the Taconic State Parkway, a winding, unlit road. And the night he spoke for forty minutes on cable TV began with his driving the car in a meandering pattern across two lanes of traffic. When I took over the wheel, he fell into a heavy sleep and stayed in a detached, otherworldly state for the rest of the evening. Yet he still managed to perform beautifully for the camera; he spoke clearly and answered questions accurately.

He always bounces back, or at least he has until now. I try to convince myself he's not as sick as his numbers suggest. Henry comments occasionally that we're both dead on paper, which we naturally consider the best way to be dead. Bill's T-cell count alone justifies Henry's comment; his count is five. (In the good old days, 1991 or 1992, when Bill had a whopping twelve T cells, he joked about six being male and six female; if so, he said, they might get horny and reproduce.)

To most people, five T cells would be a sign to take that once-in-a-lifetime trip or parcel out their possessions. However, Bill has had fewer than twenty T cells for over three years now, meaning that either T cells are overrated by the medical community or Bill's immune system is the one part of him that is uneducated, uninformed.

He had two good months after the "great sleep" ended. But he recently started experiencing cyclical fevers every Monday that make his head pound and his body exude heat like the vortex of a wildfire. Last week his temperature hit 103.5 degrees.

"How high should we let this go, Bill, before we panic?" I asked.

"Oh, a hundred and five," he said before falling back into a stupor.

Fortunately the fever had peaked and he spent the next hour throwing off his blankets and soaking the sheets with sweat.

Henry describes this as a typical "shake and bake" episode. One day not long ago I walked into the living room and found Bill sitting with a blanket and the dog covering him, his body shivering convulsively, his teeth literally crashing into each other. The dog whined and whimpered, unable to understand why Bill clattered so, and positioned himself stomach to stomach with his master, paws splayed for steadiness. He offered his warmth to the man he loves so much.

After shaking, Bill bakes with high, spiking fevers. The first such episode occurred over a year ago, when I woke up in the middle of the night to a wildly gyrating bed, as if I had been transported in my sleep to a cheap motel room. But it was Bill vibrating, not some motorized mattress. After giving him a few Benadryl capsules, I simply held him as tightly as I could and tried to will him my wellness as his fever climbed and his skin turned scarlet. For a while we lay like clacking spoons until the Benadryl made him sleep.

So now it is two-thirty in the morning and I have awakened and seen the light streaming through Bill's thighs, and I have to admit that he may be getting worse. Since I am deaf without my hearing aids, I touch him to reassure myself that he breathes. I am relieved at his clamminess; the fever has finally broken. I look at his skinny legs and wonder if he is getting that "AIDS look": cadaverous, frail.

But no, I cannot believe that Bill is slipping away from me.

I cannot believe that these words may become his eulogy.

Maybe he just needs to eat more.

Maybe his five uneducated T cells will rise to the challenge and plump him like a Thanksgiving turkey.

Maybe I should not wake up in the middle of the night and look at him.

Bitter Pill, Bitter Wind

For three years now, whenever the leaves begin to fall, the nodules begin to pop.

After a stretch of ten months with no outbreaks, after ten months of lulling myself into thinking maybe I *was* the first HIV-positive person cured of *M. haemophilum* disease; after ten months of luxuriously answering, "I'm feeling pretty good, thanks"; after ten months my T cells plummeted and, while absentmindedly scratching my left thigh, my fingers encountered a lump. A small lump, perhaps the size of a cherry, but a lump nonetheless. And with this single insignificant gesture I felt it all begin again, and I must now wonder how long and how arduous this episode will ultimately prove.

The nodules first appeared during the fall of 1990, when I rolled over on my left side one morning and incoherently thought I had been stabbed with a fork. There it was, a nodule the size of a plum that had magically ripened overnight.

Henry scheduled me for next-day surgery after he saw it, saying simply, "It must come out."

Perhaps I should have anticipated this intrusion of my body; for about a year, walking had no longer been a given. I had been diagnosed with peripheral neuropathy. By the time I found the first lump that November, I used a cane more frequently than I did not. I went into the operating room fully expecting the surgeon to find a mass, a tumor. Instead, he shouted for culture media because he had hit a huge abscess of mysterious fluid. He drained away the juice of my plum, and I walked out of the hospital without my cane. I left thinking all my problems had just been solved with a single cut. In retrospect, I probably walked out caneless only because of the lingering effects of anesthesia.

Far from eradicating my problems, the surgery proved to be just the beginning of their multiplication. I developed strange lesions on my left ear that randomly opened and drained and were excruciating to touch. They resembled herpes zoster, or shingles, but they didn't respond to zoster medications. The diagnosis changed from week to week while the disease progressed.

Then, like machine-gun fire, like nodular fission, lumps exploded all over my left side, from my toes to the tip of my ear. The facial lesions were the worst. I couldn't cover them with makeup, and I often refused to leave home and bare myself to public scrutiny. These facial eruptions evolved into running, open sores which I constantly had to pat dry with a tissue.

One morning a colleague came into my office for advice. A sensitive woman just out of school, she stood in front of me, unable to speak. Her eyes, riveted almost unwillingly to the side of my face, filled with tears as she fled my office.

I neatly plotted each new outbreak on a faceless diagram I shared with Henry each week. At one point there were over twenty active sites.

In addition to being unattractive and boillike, the lumps were extremely painful. Often I sensed them weeks before they emerged, and felt increased warmth in the area of the future nodule. I had bizarre dreams that later proved significant; once I dreamed I was shot in the arm, and a nodule appeared at the bullet's entry point within days. In another dream I whipped a newborn calf unmercifully. The next day I found a lump behind and below my left knee.

The bacterium causing the nodules strained against my skin, searched for a way to escape. When it couldn't find one, it simply continued to grow outward, sometimes until it was as large as a nectarine. The only way to alleviate the pressure building up inside was to insert a needle directly into the nodule and draw out the liquid. This procedure is called an aspiration, but it is nothing to aspire to. Week after week I lay on the examining table, fingernails digging into Bill's palm, and cursed and cried and screamed. Until this day, I am conditioned to flinch at the mere sound of a syringe drawing up fluid, even if it's not painful, even if it's not my own fluid being drawn.

As the nodules grew in size, the pain increased, and I relied upon synthetic morphines like Dilaudid— or "deluded," as a friend calls it—to transport me to foggy lands where I could no longer feel my body. I was still trying to work, and on the days when I could actually get out of bed, I had to trade painkillers for mental clarity.

One evening Bill and I went to our dentist in lower Manhattan. The pain in my legs from both my bacterial infection and my neuropathy was particularly bad and getting worse, and I was sweating and pale by the time I dropped into the dentist's chair. I barely got out again, and I walked only a few steps before Bill hailed a cab to Grand Central Station. I managed to board the train, but Bill and the conductor had to carry me off when we arrived at our stop. While Bill left to get the car, I tried to reach the stairs to the parking lot. I gripped the railing with both hands, unable to stand or move without external support. I literally dragged myself along the platform with my arms while my legs followed like lifeless sacks of flour and my eyes clouded with tears of humiliation.

Bill rescued me and allowed me to use his body as a crutch until we reached the car.

To this day, this is my most vivid memory of what pain is and can be. The human brain, however, is remarkably merciful. Although I can recount the details of this incident, I cannot remember what the pain actually felt like. Intellectually, I know it was intense, excruciating, and thus I can conclude that I don't ever want to experience it again. But my mind has kindly blocked out the actual feeling of the pain—similar, I suppose, to a mother forgetting the agony of childbirth when she sees her baby for the first time.

Perhaps this happens so we can face future pain with the strength of ignorance and not the cowardice of memory.

Meanwhile, treatment after treatment failed, test after test proved inconclusive. But we slowly closed in on the truth, that we were dealing with a class of infections called mycobacteria. Henry hypothesized that I had a subcutaneous form of tuberculosis or a strange manifestation of *mycobacterium avium complex,* one of the leading killers of people with AIDS. I expected to die, and on those days when getting out of bed was too difficult to even contemplate, I indeed wanted to die. I continued to work, but rarely put in more than a three-day week.

On October 4, 1991, Henry unexpectedly called me on the job and said, "I just got bad news from the lab. I'm going to have to put you back in."

I had already been hospitalized five times that year; my last discharge had come only three weeks earlier.

"When?" I whispered.

"Now," he said. "You have to leave now and meet me at the hospital."

I never returned to work.

The lab results had finally shown that I had *M. haemophilum,* an organism that normally ignores the human body as a host but which can present problems for people undergoing organ transplants or who are otherwise immunocompromised. It lives in water, air, and food, and its ability to cause disease is so rare that I was only the nineteenth case ever documented. Transplant patients eventually clear it when their immunity revives, but people with AIDS usually don't outlast it. Occasionally I ask Henry if he's heard of any survivors of *M. haemophilum* besides me. He usually finds something particularly compelling to study in my chart when I ask him this question, and he mumbles about lack of follow-up.

We both understand this to mean no.

Bill and I drew up our wills and visited an old, peaceful cemetery to price plots. When we passed through the gates, I paused. The first thing I saw was the tombstone of a gentleman who had died in the nineteenth century. His name was William Burns.

At that moment there seemed no clearer indication that death was coming soon. The only thing more significant for me would have been seeing my own name already engraved upon it as well.

My treatment, which had been aggressive even when we didn't have a conclusive diagnosis, now turned brutal. My veins collapsed under the constant invasion of peripheral IV lines, so I had a catheter permanently implanted in my chest. I left the hospital still needing to undergo four hours of IV infusions each day. By this time Bill was working full-time from home and also receiving IV infusions through *his* catheter. Many afternoons we sat together on the couch, each independently "dripping." We learned not to hang our medicines from the same pole after Bill, connected to his IV bag, ran for the telephone with me in tow and still connected to *my* IV bag. We obtained separate IV poles and a portable phone.

Under the appropriate treatment regimen, I improved. The time between new outbreaks of nodules extended from one day to three days to two weeks and even to a month. At long last, the lesions on my face and ear closed over, leaving me with blue-black scars that even now take half an hour to cover using a plastic spatula and thick theater-quality makeup.

Henry started calling me Wanda the Witch on those days when the pain made me look particularly wretched.

"Hi, Wanda," he'd say when I felt like hell.

Wanda still occasionally resurfaces, but less frequently. I've learned how to hide her effectively under my Dermablend.

For the first time in over a year I believed I might survive. But shortly into 1992 I felt a fullness and heard a buzzing in my ears, intermittent at first, then constant. I refused to believe that the medicine I took intravenously could cause auditory damage, refused to believe that one drug could both help me and harm me so dramatically. The likelihood of what would happen if I discontinued its use was too frightening to contemplate. So Henry and Bill and I crossed our fingers, knowing I would rather be alive and deaf than dead and unimpaired.

Around this same time, Bill and I attended a weekend workshop that promoted a "mind, heal thy body" philosophy. This philosophy seems overly simplistic to me; it makes the patient responsible for bodily processes that may be well out of his or her control. I don't mind taking responsibility for my behavior, but I think it's unfair to have to take responsibility for a virus as well.

The only significant part of the workshop for me turned out to be the answers Bill and I gave to this question: "If you had to lose either your sense of hearing or your sense of sight, which would you prefer to lose?"

Bill, who spends much of his time in front of a computer screen and who suffers from CMV retinitis, a condition that often causes blindness, said he would rather lose his hearing.

I, who play the piano and regard the spoken word as so important, and who is on ototoxic medications, chose to lose my vision.

Bill already acts as my interpreter in many situations; he is my ears. I fear the day will come when I will read the newspaper to him: I will be his eyes.

The buzzing grew worse. It was February, piercingly cold. I lay in bed one night and shook uncontrollably.

"What's wrong?" Bill asked, reaching over to quiet me.

"I'm going deaf and I'm terrified!" I cried.

"You're not going to lose your hearing, you're not, you're not." Bill repeated the words like a mantra, unable to do anything to eliminate the buzzing or the fear, unable to reverse the damage already done.

The next morning I turned on our electronic scale and waited for the beep to tell me to step up. I waited and waited: no beep. I looked down; the zero was flashing as usual. I asked Bill to bring new batteries, not realizing that the LED wouldn't light up if the batteries were dead. Bill tested the scale and announced that nothing was wrong.

"But the beep . . ." I began, and then it hit me: the scale worked, but my ears did not. The beep existed in a high-frequency world now lost to me.

I ultimately lost over 50 percent of my hearing in both ears. But the Amikacin, toxic as it was, had done its antibacterial job well, and I switched to oral medications to keep the *M. haemophilum* more or less under control. I entered a truly happy time, one in which nodules appeared infrequently.

My last major outbreak occurred during the Thanksgiving holidays a year ago and persisted until the beginning of the new year. It was severe, and pointed to a major relapse. What could we do? I was already on Henry's "haemophilum cocktail"; the only thing left to do was increase the dosage of one of my medicines. I became a one-woman experiment studying the effects of rifabutin at four times the normal FDA-approved dose.

For the last ten months this strategy has worked, and I have been completely nodule-free. This high dose, combined with all my other medications, has wreaked havoc on my system; I discontinued all medications in September after vomiting blood. A month passed with no outbreaks.

I've done it, I thought, I've cleared these damn bacteria.

At the end of the second month of my medicine-free holiday, at the end of a ten-month pain-free stretch, I made the mistake of scratching my thigh. I discovered that I hadn't cleared it after all, that this bacterium was under my skin the whole time, hiding, gathering up enough force to erupt and shatter my few months of wonderful delusion. Two more nodules have since appeared, and I now face the prospect of a bone marrow biopsy, the worst kind of needle aspiration I can imagine, one that will pierce my very core. One that, I suspect, will introduce me to a pain I have not yet experienced.

M. haemophilum is an insidious killer that thrives on low temperatures, perhaps even on flesh growing colder as death approaches. It attacks the coldest parts of me, my distant portions—arms, legs, face. I used to fear its invasion into my private parts, but my vagina, my buttocks, my breasts, are all seats of warmth in my body, and protect me. Can it enter my brain? I sometimes wonder. Or is the heat of my passion and my thoughts stronger than even this cold-blooded killer?

This bacterium, my bacterium, seems to come out of hibernation fully when a white shroud of snow covers the ground, when the leaves crunch like brittle bones underfoot. Although I revive a bit when the temperature increases, it is inaccurate to say that I have never had a nodule in August or that I have been perfectly well when my skin absorbs the hot life of the sun. But my condition improves markedly during these times. It is now clear to me, the paranoid host, that during the spring and the summer *M. haemophilum* simply plays a waiting game, teasing me into complacency, biding its time until the first frost in order to encapsulate my first shiver in a nodule.

This seasonal theory of my disease hasn't been proven medically, but it is what I and my mother and my sisters believe, and so I think it must be true.

And so it has waited patiently through the spring and the summer; it has allowed me to live and move freely, and now I must step back and allow it its season, allow it to live and move freely throughout my body. And to live and move with *M. haemophilum* requires days like today, which went something like this:

I lie on the examining table in Henry's office, one hand covering my eyes, one hand holding on to Bill. I wait for the first cut. What comes instead is a piercing needle prick that quickly pours beautiful anesthesia into the area above my knee.

Henry pokes the area with his fingers. "Can you feel that?" he asks. If I nod, he waits patiently, sensitive to pain as only a nonsurgeon can be. Finally he pokes and I shake my head: no sensation.

I turn to the wall and try not to cry; although I have no pain, I anticipate pain. Henry is happy with the first cut; he motions for Bill and Lydia to look deep inside my leg.

"*This* is what has been hurting her!" he says, and plucks out a pea-sized lump with an angry red center and places it gently on the specimen towel. The procedure interests Bill, and he wonders if he should have applied to medical school.

A minute later he sinks into a chair, nauseated, and decides that business school was indeed the better choice.

Pluck, pluck, Henry finds more little peas, but it is impossible to tell at this point whether they contain bacteria or simply fat deposits. I am getting free liposuction, I think, but then he scores big: two nodules with the blue centers characteristic of *M. haemophilum*. I am desperately disappointed: I had prayed for benign lipomas, not bacteria-ridden lumps.

"If it looks like a duck . . ." Henry says.

I understand.

I am still not in pain, but am nervous as always around needles, blood, knives; my nerves inspired Henry long ago to coin me "Miss Muffet." My legs quiver uncontrollably; Bill raises his head from between his legs and asks if someone put a quarter in my slot without his permission. We laugh, and the tension breaks for a moment until pluck, pluck, more peas are removed. We determine that human fat resembles turkey fat to a remarkable degree.

An hour later a dozen or more peas are lined up on the towel, prisoners of war under the control of a ruthless general. Henry now takes thick black thread and laces up my wounds like a boot; I will have a battle scar resembling a lightning bolt, or a hockey stick. Lying on the table in my underwear, legs spread, I think: I must either get rid of all my short skirts or buy some opaque stockings. Then it is done, but my legs still shake and Bill and Henry ask me why, and I shrug. But I think it is anger and hate that make me shake, the same raw emotions that make my voice quaver when I am pressed unwillingly into an argument. If *M. haemophilum* personified rose up in front of me, I would kill it dead without hesitation and kick its mortally wounded flesh with the same disdain it exhibits toward me when the winds turn bitter.

This is how much I hate it.

My specimens were photographed and preserved, and Bill and I drove my disembodied nodules to the lab; we must now wait several weeks for the results. *M. haemophilum* grows excruciatingly slowly. I finally met the woman who has personally analyzed little parts of me for over three years; she didn't seem to know what to say to the whole person she encountered. I shook her hand, but also was tongue-tied, so I simply gave her my pieces and left.

Most of the leaves have fallen by now, but I sense the first snow approaching, sense it in the scattered spots of warmth on my legs and arms, sense it in the way I have begun to move, slowly, painfully, like an old woman.

Sense it in revived dreams of arrows and bullets and whips.

Sense it in the cooling of a body that still lives.

Thoughts I Never Had

December 26, 1993 _____

I never thought about ice; it miraculously appeared in trays for my taking; it magically regenerated in time for my nightly glass of ice water. You wrought this miracle wordlessly.* You are not here with me tonight, and the ice cube trays are empty.

I never thought about what to do if the top of the soda bottle was too tight. I could hand it over to you, and my dryness would be quenched. But you are not here with me tonight, and I thirst.

I never thought about the houseplants; you invisibly kept them from dying, you nourished them with food. But you are

*Beginning in December 1993, Bill was hospitalized almost continuously. I addressed most of my subsequent writings to him, hoping to say on paper what was becoming increasingly difficult to say in person.

not here tonight, and, like the plants, I hunger for your return.

I never thought about actually losing you. You always recovered; you always seemed stronger with each challenge. But now you do not recover. You destroy your cells like before, but don't regenerate them. You are tired and weak from fighting insidious attackers, from fighting the effects of substances meant to save you.

I never thought about spending all my evenings alone. I sleep only on my side of the bed, because the other side is yours.

I sit only at my own place at the table, because the other place is yours.

I do not use your toothpaste, do not eat your Fig Newtons or your cherry Italian ices. I superstitiously leave them untouched, thinking that leaving them untouched will cause you to enter the room, refill trays, open bottles, water plants.

You sleep on my left side, near my heart; you warm me.

But you are not here with me tonight, and my heart breaks, and I am cold.

In my nightstand drawer, tied with a shoelace, are the letters Bill and I wrote to each other from 1983 through 1985. In August 1994, I took them to Bill's hospital room and read them aloud to him.

Some of these letters seem strangely significant when I read them again.

Most of them are just the silly ramblings of two kids in love, two kids who must have lived in another lifetime.

Here are a few excerpts. Note the way Bill signed the first letter. While still engaged, we struggled to decide what last name we would use once we were married. We thought about hyphenating both our last names, but then would it be Burns-O'Reilly or O'Reilly-Burns? We considered creating a new name that would be ours alone. We eventually succumbed to tradition, but this letter is Bill's tongue-in-cheek response to our dilemma. (His legal name actually contains the Roman numeral VI; I used to tease him that his name was bigger than he was.)

July 7, 1984

To my dearest, most sweetest Bubaloo . . .

I was just about to start whining about how bored I am and how I want to come home. . . . [Why] do I conclude that I am bored? Simply put, because we are not together!!! How, with one million and one things to do, can one be bored? It's just not logical (but what really is logical?) I'll have you know, Ms. O'Reilly, that no one has ever made me feel at all like this. Separation from [others] was freedom; now it's just plain hell. Anyone who could bring a tear to the eye and lump to the throat of this hard-hearted, cold, unfeeling, logical automaton of a programmer is certainly a very special person and YOU MAY ALREADY HAVE WON A GORGEOUS DIAMOND ENGAGEMENT RING! . . .

Love,
William H. O'Reilly VI

January 1, 1985

(From Bill's list of New Year's resolutions)
#7: Survive without an ulcer.

January 17, 1985

Dearest Bill,

. . . I had a strange dream that you were chasing me around holding a scab in your hand, threatening to stick it on me. (It was very foul-looking.) It must mean something. . . . Am I refusing to fully heal from a wound (symbolic, of course!) . . . ? Do you have a hidden fantasy of seeing me covered with open, running sores (yuck!)? . . . When I figure it out, I'll tell you. . . .

Always,
Janice

March 11, 1985

Dearest Bill,

   How are you feeling? Shall I send you some rubber panties . . . or are [your present intestinal difficulties] so much better that there is no need for such humiliating accessories? Now that the worst is over, I must tell you that you really had me worried! I had awful visions of you slipping into a coma from 106-degree fever, or being hospitalized for a rare disease. . . . Please try to take care of yourself!

Always,
Janice

P.S. Kiss, kiss, kiss, hug, hug, hug!!!

PART EIGHT: 1994

I opened for my lover,
        but my lover had left; he was gone.
        My heart sank at his departure.
I looked for him but did not find him.
        I called him but he did not answer.

                                Song of Songs 5:6

Life Fragments

I.

A friend recently commented, "Why, this book isn't really about AIDS at all. It's actually a love story."

When I repeated this, you laughed, and said, "Right. Boy meets girl. Boy kills girl. And don't forget the first part: Boy meets boy. Boy kills boy."

II.

We met on a hot June day at Oberlin College, two of the elite, two of thirty or so students chosen nationwide to be part of an international research program. Our projects were all socially minded: rural access to health care, computers for

handicapped kids, rape crisis theory, and so on. We were
1980s students who would have been 1960s Peace Corps
volunteers.

When I first saw you, I immediately thought of Tom
Cruise or Gene Kelly. I was particularly impressed with your
nose, so fine and straight, like a Greek statue. I was also impressed with your hair, so thick and wavy, and your brows,
so perfectly arched. That night, with me at the keyboard, the
group gathered around the piano for a sing-along. You
turned my pages for me that night. You've been turning them
for me ever since.

III.

We traveled together back to New York after that conference, and I lied and told you I didn't like landings, and you
held my hand for the first time. You kept holding it as we
stepped from the plane and passed through the gate.

You said, "I have everything I want," and squeezed.

Then we both went home, you thinking you had just acquired a girlfriend, me thinking about the boy I had been dat-
ing for years. You kept calling me; I kept calling you. And I
stayed with my boyfriend, who, although fully a foot taller
than you, did not quite measure up anymore.

IV.

We wanted to be together, but I wasn't brave enough to
end my old, tired relationship, and you weren't brave enough
to show me how old and tired it was. I think you must have
viewed my decision as a rejection from the entire female
race. So you called up a computer bulletin board and found a
club close to home, and met a guy whose last name you nc

onger remember. You called me at work to tell me that you
hought you might be gay; I thought I had lost you forever.
Soon after your relationship ended, we surrendered to the in-
evitable. We have been stuck to each other like hot tar to
sneakers for eleven years now.

But my two months of vacillation were the two months
that changed our lives, in effect ended our lives.

How long will I torture myself by asking "What if?"

I think until I die.

V.

Was there ever such a time as we had in London, those
first months of discovery and beginnings and passion? We
were so pretentious: we ate fish and chips, we drank sherry.
We shared a flat with another student but ignored him and
preferred to play our own private game of house. We pretended we were married because we wanted so badly to be. It
was as impossible then as it is now for us to imagine living
without each other.

VI.

You borrowed money from your father and bought a ring
and proposed. We originally planned a traditional wedding—
lots of guests, big reception, music, attendants, the works—
but it didn't feel right; it almost felt like a mockery of who we
were. So we had a small celebration, fuss-free, a modest party
at my parents' apartment after the ceremony. We are the only
couple we know who chose not to go the traditional route.

Then again we're the only couple we know who has
AIDS.

Although we didn't know it at the time.

VII.

I don't remember much from our first year. I think we were perfectly happy; I think we went through all the normal pains and contortions that go hand in hand with married life. I got angry with you when you put in too many hours at work; you got angry with me when I forgot to balance the checkbook. We established routines: The *Times* and too many pastries from the bakery every Sunday morning. Laundry done every two weeks with little attention paid to proper sorting and none to folding underwear. After all, who cared if our underwear was wrinkled? A huge trip to the grocery store every month that cost hundreds of dollars because we couldn't be bothered to shop more frequently. We still live in these rhythms, although we started folding our underwear after your grandmother shamed us into it.

We relaxed into normalcy. I remember only one major disagreement that first year, although I've long forgotten the reason for it. I remember losing my temper and throwing a dictionary at you. We both laughed when I did this, and I still have a redheaded temper, although you no longer duck when it shows itself. In the last eleven years we have had two or three arguments; we've never stayed mad at each other for more than an hour or two. Or rather I've never stayed mad; you never seem to get angry in return. In all these years you have never once raised your voice to me.

VIII.

When first diagnosed HIV-positive, I reeled from anger. Anger at God, at injustice, at you. I tried not to let you see it but I don't know if I succeeded. I struggled to be supportive struggled for us to present a unified front to the world, al-

...ough I still found AIDS embarrassing. Or rather I found its ...ource in our lives embarrassing.

In addition, I felt stupid for thinking that AIDS could only ...appen to people who frequented shooting galleries or bath-...ouses. Idiotic for refusing to acknowledge that anyone, no ...atter how kind, no matter how smart, no matter how much ...happened to love him, could be unlucky enough to acquire ...virus.

During the first six months after diagnosis I tried to main-...ain my equanimity, be strong and mature, although at ...wenty-three I had to work hard to possess these traits. But ...ne day it became too much for me, and I asked, "Didn't you ...now that you could get AIDS? What in God's name made ...ou do something so dangerous?"

You looked at me, not even angry, not even hurt by my ...mplied accusation, and simply replied, "Nobody told me ...bout it. I didn't know."

At first I wanted you to apologize, take the blame upon ...ourself, beg me for forgiveness. I could see in your eyes ...en, as I can now, your sorrow, your sadness, your love for ...e, your regret. But it took me a long time to acknowledge ...at apologies can only be given for deliberate actions.

You never meant to hurt me.

This is why I no longer need to hear the words: "I'm ...orry."

Friends

We recently visited our friend Danny in the intensive care unit. He had been in the hospital for almost a month, but his move to the ICU followed the removal of a four-centimeter tumor from his brain. We expected to find the charming flight attendant we had first met two years ago. Instead, we found a man-child: a man in the knowledge of his mortality, a child in his complete dependence on others for life itself.

Danny looked like a dying man to me. Over the years I have reluctantly learned to recognize the signs of imminent death: a blurring of the body's boundaries, a gentle and sometimes not-so-gentle fusion with surrounding elements, a sigh into oblivion.

I used to be devastated by my encounters with dying friends and routinely prayed for miracles to save them. Today I am more likely to pray for God to take my friends sooner rather than later or, at the very least, to take them painlessly.

Danny's decline was accompanied by occasional moments of lucidity and a stubborn re-emergence of the person he once was. On this particular evening Bill alerted him to our presence by loudly announcing our names as we entered his room.

Danny jumped and said: "Sir!" as if he were serving on a Boeing 747 and a first-class passenger needed him.

"They're trying to starve me; this is such shit food," he said as we entered.

On his tray was a plate covered with stuffed pasta shells, which Danny scooped into his mouth with his hands; he ignored his cutlery. His blue bib was covered with sauce, the result of midair collisions between plate and mouth. He finally picked up the entire container and simply tried to pour his supper into himself.

"How are you two? You doing all right?" he asked.

We replied, "Fine, just fine," and Danny nodded and babbled a few incoherent sentences.

Thirty seconds later, he repeated, "How are you doing? Are you doing okay?"

"Fine, Danny, we're fine," we said.

"So, are you guys doing all right?" came a moment later, as if it were an entirely new question.

I don't know what painkiller Danny had been given. Maybe the medicine confused him. I don't know how much a four-centimeter tumor impairs a person's brain. I do know that Danny was losing his mind, and he was losing it with all his natural aplomb.

"We're going to San Diego next week," I said, searching for a topic to penetrate Danny's confusion. I had found one.

"San Diego, wonderful city. Very nice, really very nice."

Then that bit of conversation ended and he resumed the task of pasta-pouring.

I tried again. "We just came from seeing Dr. Frey," I said.

Danny had been Henry's patient for about a year. By the

time Henry met him, however, Danny was already on his final descent.

"We just came from his office," I continued, and something clicked.

"You just saw Dr. Frey?" Danny said. "Is he still awake?"

We couldn't help it; we laughed.

"What did you say?" Bill chuckled.

"Dr. Frey, is he still awake?" Danny repeated. We assured him that he was indeed awake and seeing patients as we spoke.

"Good, good," he said. "I have to talk to him about this," and gestured around the room with a look of disgust. Henry would get a garbled earful later that night for sure—that is, if Danny remembered who Henry was, or why he wanted to speak with him.

We left thinking we would never see Danny again, at least not the quick-witted motor-mouth we once knew, the person who would gladly tell you his life story after knowing you only five minutes.

We were right; he died a week later. Danny is the seventh friend we have lost to AIDS in the past year, and the twentieth to date. This may not seem like a lot of dead friends to some people, to residents of neighborhoods where gunfire is background music, or to members of the gay community who have already seen hundreds fall. But before AIDS, I never would have been able to come up with twenty living people I would even consider friends, never mind come up with twenty deceased ones. But these twenty people from my AIDS life were friends in the truest sense of the word, people I could call not on the basis of an old shared association but rather on the basis of a new shared disease.

Danny was our twentieth friend to die of AIDS. Ten years ago our friend Jack had died; we now think that he also was HIV-infected.

During my senior year in college, I received a phone call.

"Jack died yesterday," said the voice on the other end.

"What?" I cried. I couldn't believe it. Jack was a gentle intellectual man who loved his students and pushed them to be activists for social change. He was part of the international program in which Bill and I participated. I liked Jack and regarded him as a mentor.

I was asked to eulogize him at a memorial service. I agreed, then asked: "What was the cause of death?"

After a protracted pause, I heard the response.

"Pneumonia."

I took the reply at face value, although I wondered why such a treatable illness had killed a middle-aged man in 1984.

I delivered the eulogy, replete with clichés about Jack the role model, Jack the independent thinker, Jack the inspiration for future generations. During the service I sat next to Jack's longtime lover and occasionally squeezed his hand. Afterward the mourners dispersed; Bill and I went to see *The Fantasticks*, playing nearby. We sat close to the stage, and when the male lead appeared, we almost fell off our chairs; he was the spitting image of Jack. Coming on the heels of his memorial service, it seemed a strange sign of unknown meaning.

To this day I think of Jack whenever I hear the song "Try to Remember."

Two or three years after our diagnoses, I had a revelation while doing routine housework.

Pneumonia. Gay. My God, I thought. Jack died of AIDS!

I wonder if I would have changed my eulogy had I known then what I now believe to have been the cause of Jack's death. The answer is probably yes, and my eulogy probably would have suffered for it. It was already trite, and I probably would have transformed Jack into a stereotypical AIDS victim. It is undoubtedly better that my eulogy ignored

AIDS; my ignorance compelled me, at least, to talk about Jack the person, not Jack the virus.

But, oh, the eulogy I could deliver today if given a second chance.

After Jack, our friends with AIDS dissolved like ice sculptures at a banquet, slowly at first, then more rapidly with time's passage. First it was Mark, whom we nicknamed "Sergio" for his flashy designer sweat suits. Mark suffered from a form of Kaposi's sarcoma that started in his lungs and subsequently went systemic. Right before his death we sent him a pamphlet with a butterfly, which symbolized hope and renewal on its cover. In return, Mark sent us a carefully framed paper napkin with a butterfly design. He died a few weeks later.

Timothy, wise, spiritual, and beloved, followed soon after. When I visited him in a New York hospital, I asked how long he'd been in during this particular stay.

"Haven't I always been here?" he replied.

"I love you, girl," he said as I left, the final words of our final conversation.

Timothy's funeral was held at a monastery in upstate New York. After a service of loudly sung spirituals and effusive public remembrances, the mourners went to the dining hall while the casket was removed. The chapel bells chimed joyously.

Weeks later the priest who had presided at the service telephoned. We chatted for a while, then he asked, "Do you remember how the bells rang at the end of Timothy's funeral?"

I replied, "Yes, they were beautiful."

"You know, Tim really loved those bells," he said. "He loved hearing them ring on Sunday morning. So after his funeral I wanted to thank whoever rang them.

"But I checked with every one here, and not one of them arranged for the bells to ring. We even looked for mechanical problems, but everything checked out."

He paused.

"It was as if the bells themselves decided to give Timothy their own final tribute."

Who was next? I believe it was Harry, the good-looking construction worker who was a wonderful flirt. Harry, who stayed by his best friend's side while he underwent chemotherapy. Harry, whose muscular body was later eaten away by his own bout with cancer, and who shaved his head so that he wouldn't have to watch his hair fall out. He didn't realize at the time that the abdominal radiation he was to receive doesn't necessarily cause hair loss. Harry, who religiously played the same three numbers every day, but who never really hit the jackpot.

Although he probably would say he struck gold with HIV.

I wonder if he ever played his T-cell count?

I last saw the old Elizabeth, the vigorous Elizabeth, at a mutual friend's funeral. She was Timothy's female counterpart: soft-spoken, loving, infinitely kind. She died gently, unobtrusively, last summer, and had a big Baptist funeral attended by hundreds.

It was my first such funeral, and Elizabeth's open casket reposed at the foot of the altar. White-gloved church ladies attended the family, poured glasses of water, set up folding chairs, waved away the heat with paper fans. The minister closed the casket at the end of the service, and the women in the congregation screamed, their wails piercing even the farthest reaches of the choir loft where we sat. They yelled and keened like women from another country, another century. If I'd been less white than most of my fellow mourners, less reserved, I would have joined their piercing lament.

I left the church, voice intact, a purse full of damp tissues the only evidence of my grief.

Meg finally died last July after dying slowly for eleven years. A mother figure to many, she dispensed practical advice on treatments, doctors, and living while dying.

I never once heard her ask, "Why me?"

Meg liked control, and meticulously planned her memorial service, which included many readings, testimonies, and a total of seventeen songs. We sat sweltering on a day that broke the hundred-degree mark and silently cursed Meg's timing while, at the same time, we were impressed that she'd had the last word in true Meg style.

And then there was Alice. My closest friend with AIDS, she was someone with whom I spoke several times a week for over three years. Two hundred fifty pounds when we first met, Alice was ten years my senior and full of hell. At the time of her death, she was so thin her body lay as flat as a sheet of paper.

Alice experienced neuropathy so severe that she slowly stopped feeling her body; at the end, all that was left of her was her smile. I think of her as my Cheshire Cat.

I dream of Alice often, but never as the heavy cherub she was when healthy, though that is how I'd like to remember her. Instead, I picture her as the bone-thin, profoundly sad woman she was during her last days.

In my dreams, Alice looks at me with pleading eyes, and I give her useless potions and pills. Or she says again to me, as she did on the last day I saw her: "I'm so cold, I'm so cold."

In my dreams, I pile blankets on top of her and wrap her as tightly as a mummy, only to watch her shiver more violently, suffering from a deep, abiding coldness my blankets can't fix.

There are others who have already died, others about whose death I have yet to learn. They all have their stories, although I cannot separate them from the HIV that bound us together. I wish I had known each of them pre-AIDS, although we probably would have walked right past each other in our former lives.

I was surprised to learn at Timothy's funeral that he had four children; he never mentioned them to me, and I wonder if they played much of a role in his dying life. I never asked Alice if she went to her prom or cheated on a test; I do know she dreamed of having children one day, although she was already over forty when she died. I don't know how Elizabeth rose through the ranks of a major corporation at a time when neither blacks nor women became executives.

I lack knowledge of these nonviral details, but it doesn't matter. I love each of them, regardless.

My eulogies here provide only snapshots of lives filled with images. But if I could deliver a eulogy for all my deceased friends, this is the eulogy I would give:

These were my friends.

They had lives, wives, husbands, children, sisters, brothers, lovers, mothers, fathers. They could have been your wife, husband, child, sister, brother, lover, mother, or father.

They craved life's romance, although they had an unromantic disease. They dreamed about the future, and they imagined themselves in the future about which they dreamed.

They weren't bad. Like all of us, they did some bad and some good.

They were as different from one another as students in a lecture hall. They came from varied ethnic and racial backgrounds, all kinds of religions and different sexual orientations. Some of them went public with their disease. Some of them had a hard time even admitting to themselves that they were sick.

They didn't set out to become infected with HIV. They didn't want to have AIDS.

They didn't deserve to die as they did.

They dreamed of a cure.

They wanted to live.

Stillness

I should have stayed in bed that morning. It was October 16, 1992, a day during one of the most beautiful autumns I can remember, when you would swear the trees had brightness knobs turned up to their highest points. Stained-glass reds, crackling oranges, yellows and browns side by side as on well-done fried eggs, colors jumping out in stark relief against the gray, drizzly sky.

It was the last day Bill worked before leaving his job on disability. It also happened to be the day I should have died but for some reason did not.

Bill and I rose early. He was anxious to put in a full day at work and resolve any lingering loose ends. I had to chair a committee meeting at nine. Tears sprang into my eyes when Bill pulled out of the driveway in his rickety Datsun, brief-case on the passenger seat. A part of our world ended then;

in the future we would have to file these nine-to-five days under "Memories."

Nostalgia slowed me down that morning, and I, always either on time or early, ran dangerously late. I pulled on a skirt and blazer, artifacts of my own working days, and swallowed a bowl of cereal with my morning pills. One last glance in the mirror revealed blond eyelashes; I had somehow skipped a step in my long-established foundation-eyeliner-mascara-eyebrows routine. I stomped into the bathroom and took deep breaths to keep my temper in check while I fixed the problem. I now had half an hour to get to a meeting that was a forty-five-minute drive from home.

Raincoat on, purse in hand, hair and face palatable for outside consumption, I opened the door to leave. Such an unappreciated and simple act, really, this act of door opening. Hand to knob, a twist, a gentle push or pull, and you're out. There is nothing inherently dramatic about it—unless, of course, you happen to be the owner of a hyperactive puppy.

I opened the door, and Puggy, our almost-housebroken pug, hurled himself between my legs and escaped. Puggy, who never did and never does come when called, decided that my chasing him was a thrilling and unexpected game. He ran in wide looping circles around the house, around me, onto the road, into the woods. I tried to coax him into the car by patting the seat next to me as if this was the one and only place in the world he should want to be. I bribed him with pieces of American cheese arranged in a line leading to the front door, Hansel and Gretel–style.

I yelled, I threatened, I pleaded. I needed to leave but couldn't, because I knew if I left him alone he would be hit by a car or be sold to a research lab or fall into some other horrible misfortune.

It began to rain. I backed the car down the driveway with the door open, hoping Pug would jump in. Instead, he ran directly behind the car, naively trusting that I wouldn't roll him out flat like pie dough. When all my efforts failed, I simply sat down on the wooden steps leading to our front door and cried, a Kraft singles in my hand.

The lure of the cheese finally became too much, and Pug inched forward until I could grab his collar. I picked him up, yelling "Bad dog! Bad dog!" and spanked his bottom mercilessly. He looked at me with his round brown puppy eyes and whimpered, not understanding why this normally wonderful creature, this huge two-legged plaything whose eyes he licked open every morning, should so suddenly and swiftly turn on him. But at that moment on that day I didn't care what he thought. I had murder in my heart.

I put Pug behind the portable gate blocking off the kitchen. Finally I slammed and locked the front door and got into the car, which after six years we finally owned, having made the last payment the previous week. I now had ten minutes to get to a meeting forty-five minutes away.

My path that morning took me on a slick, winding road. Still teary-eyed, I said over and over to myself, "Stay calm. He's only a dumb dog. The meeting can't start without you."

"Breathe, breathe," I intoned, remembering how my sister and I did a "cool down" exercise after our aerobics class.

Breathe, breathe.

I am a fast driver under normal circumstances and a faster driver when upset. But I kept after myself to relax, tried to stay within the speed limit, and looked down at the gas gauge: empty. I pulled into the nearest station, aggravated at having to pay $1.61 a gallon. Tank full, I set out again, with five minutes to get to a meeting still thirty minutes away.

The roads were deserted; rush hour had come and gone without me. To my left was the Catholic monastery with its large roadside crucifix. Local folklore says that a certain truck driver stops here every morning and, rain or shine, kneels in front of this cross to pray. Immediately beyond the monastery the road dips and curves sharply to the right. Realizing I was taking the curve a little too quickly, I hit the brakes. They didn't engage, or perhaps they locked, or maybe I applied them too late. In any event, instead of slowing down, I sped up and lost control of the car.

I zoomed across the oncoming traffic lane, unable to do anything except cry, "No, no!"

I saw a telephone pole looming ahead, firm, unmoving, bigger than any pole had a right to be. Several thoughts occurred to me quick as an eye-blink. First I pictured Bill eating dinner by himself and buying for one at ShopRite, just Bill and that damn dog bouncing off the walls of our big house like two lonely pinballs ricocheting off the bumpers.

Next I wondered how my body would look after being extricated with the Jaws of Life. Whether there would be an arm where a leg used to be, or whether I'd realize my mother's oft-repeated wish: eyes in the back of my head.

And I thought, Screw you, God, you bastard, for making me live with AIDS but killing me in a car wreck. I looked at the telephone pole, I felt the car's momentum, and I knew I was going to die. And I crashed head-on into that pole and into the stone wall beside it at forty miles an hour in a mighty clash of shredding tires, crunching metal, and my own screams.

And then it was over, the car half of its original size, the entire driver's side crunched like a recycled can. I crawled out of the passenger side door—or was it the window—intent on escaping before the car exploded, which is what I thought cars always did in accidents. I flapped my arms and ran down the road with my black raincoat whipping about, a big flustered bird yelling, "Help me!" at passing cars. Within a minute a volunteer ambulance worker appeared and took my pulse and felt for broken bones. He gently touched the purple scars on my face, thinking they were from the accident, but I just shook my head no, no, too weary to explain further. A car pulled over, and the driver handed me his car

phone. I only made one call, to cancel my meeting. I decided
to call Bill once I was safe at home.

A policeman arrived within minutes. He looked at the car,
he looked at me. I was absolutely unharmed: no blood, no
bruises, not even the tiniest scratch on my body. He shook
his head. "I don't know why you're still alive. I should be
scraping you up off the road right now, lady."

He made his report and cited poor road drainage under
"cause." A tow truck hauled away the totaled car, and the
cop drove me home, chattering the whole time about his own
recent accident, the one where he landed in traction after a
drunk driver broke his back. The drive-way looked sadly barren when we pulled in.

I unlocked the door and removed Puggy's gate. I apologized for spanking him and kissed his furry face. I then
called Bill and managed to sputter, "I've been in a terrible
accident, but I'm okay. The car's gone, it's totaled.

"I'm okay," I repeated, as much for myself as for him.

He left the office immediately, at ten-thirty in the morning
of the last day he would ever work. He said his boss just
shook his head sadly when Bill told him why he had to leave
so soon after he'd arrived.

My mother stayed with me until Bill got home. She made
a cup of tea for me and let me recount the accident: how the
road curved, how I'd felt as if I were on a kiddie ride where
you pretend to steer although the path is preordained. Once
or twice I saw her eyes fill with tears; I wonder if she felt a
foreboding of another day, that future day when she would
again come face to face with the loss of her youngest child.

When Bill came home, we went to see the car, still connected to the tow truck at the auto body shop.

"Jesus," was all he said.

We drove back home in stunned silence.

We bought a new car, large and sturdy and equipped with
antilock brakes, dual airbags, and lots of steel to keep me

safe from telephone poles. I would have bought a Sherman
tank had one been available. Several months passed before I
could drive without my hands shaking, and several more before I could think calmly about that day. But when I finally
could think about it, I made an unexpected discovery.

For the hundredth time I pondered the circumstances of
the accident. I finally could admit I never should have gotten
into the car in the first place. I was already dangerously upset
from my incident with the dog. That fact, combined with
drizzly skies and curvy roads, set me up for disaster. In retrospect, I could easily understand why and how the accident
occurred.

What I couldn't understand was how I managed to survive
it unscathed.

Think, I told myself. Breathe. As I did on the morning of
the accident, I took deep breaths, hoping to re-create the one
moment that had made the difference between life and death
on a cool autumn day.

Suddenly I felt the soft velour seat against my thighs, the
grooved wheel under my hands. Once again I traveled south
and passed the monastery. I glanced down at the speedome-
ter: forty-three miles per hour. Slow down, I thought, the
speed limit here is thirty-five. The car in front of me pulled
away; the rearview mirror showed me to be alone. I hit the
brake as the road curved sharply to the right, but the wheels
never turned with the road. Instead, I heard the sound of a
thousand shrieking birds, and the car flew straight ahead.

For some reason there were no cars in the opposite lane.
There seemed to be no cars anywhere; it was almost as if I
were alone in the world for a moment, in a place and time reserved exclusively for my special clash with the beyond. I
saw the telephone pole and flashed back to an accident I'd
witnessed when I was five years old: a Volkswagen wrapped
around a tree like a spring stretched over a pencil. As a child,
had wondered if the driver's body inside also coiled simi-

larly around the tree. Today, twenty-five years later, my car felt like that Volkswagen.

I screamed.

Then, in that split second, in that moment I had not been able to remember before, I realized I was not alone in my car. I heard, or perhaps just sensed, a whisper.

"Be still."

As the car sped forward, I heard that whisper and felt—how can I say this and still sound sane?—a hand on each shoulder, two hands pressing down gently but firmly, keeping my body perfectly still, perfectly intact through the collision of steel and wood.

That is what happened. A three-second interval when the boundary between this world and the next briefly shimmered. When I heard a simple command: "Be still."

When I felt strong and insistent hands protecting me from myself, as loving and firm as the hands of a parent.

Bill's Sojourn

It used to be that windows were transparent and pages were lined and chairs could be sat upon and beds were for sleep.

These things are no longer, cannot be again. Now a rug feels like concrete and a pillow is a stone whose edges serrate my scalp. Now music is the sound of a scream, a single lonely note in the universe.

I never knew anything before.

I do not know anything now.

My body says sleep, but I will not sleep: I fear I will dream I am alone. As long as I can look at you, you will not dare to leave me, you will not dare avoid my gaze.

This is how it was: You were driving, and then you asked me to drive. We switched sides, and I turned my head as I slid behind the wheel, and I saw that you were falling. All I saw was your eye-whites, and I heard that sucking of the vortex. I felt the quivering of shock and saw your body convulse, and I thought you were dying. I saw you go somewhere without me, and I did not see angels or light around you; I was not comforted. Instead, I saw only a wet glistening hole. I pulled you back into the car and slammed the door.

You left me as instantly as a balloon escapes when a hand opens and does not close again quickly enough.

Please.

Don't go.

I thought of my plastic jug of Lourdes water, given to me by a kind priest, and I wanted to baptize you, wash you in a miracle, pour salvation into your veins.

A dead bird lies on the front lawn, fallen from a tree or knocked from its branches. Every day pieces of this bird scatter farther and farther apart until it no longer resembles a bird. It is now just a collection of feathers and bones and organs that once lived.

Please.

Don't go.

Grace is given to those who don't seek it, to those who refuse it and resist it with every cell, knowing life without it is still life, but grace without life is just air. To hell with grace; let me touch a body. Let me gaze into your eyes and die with you. Let us grasp the earth to the very end.

No, a wolf's howl to the moon. Life does not end at twenty-nine. Life does not end at an intersection. Life does not end with the words: "I think you'd better drive."

Life does not.

White as sun-bleached sand, blue as a Bermuda sea, you rock and crash and erode, and I can only watch the progress. It is larger than me. It is evolution.

Don't go, come back.

After I pulled you back into the car, I drove the two blocks to the hospital, two blocks as wide as two continents, and I heard a whisper, a gurgle, a word. Yes, a word.

My name.

I floored the gas pedal, and soon you were lifted into a chair and I was alone in a cold corridor, looking at electrified doors opening and closing, seeing with each open and close a glimpse of your cubicle. I saw blue scrubs and machines and bags of blood. The doors opened and closed; the doors went in and out like a breathing chest.

I must have aged a hundred years, or perhaps you aged a hundred years coming and going like that, but we were no longer the same age, and the nurse thought us brother and sister, not husband and wife.

Yes, we are of the same blood.

The doctor asked, "Should we revive him if necessary?"

I cried. We had talked about it once, but it was only words; it wasn't real.

So yes, he would want to be revived. At least I want him revived. I don't care what it takes. Just let me look in his eyes so I know he is here.

Don't go.

But they didn't have to bring you back; you didn't leave after all.

Somehow you are alive.

Desperate Bottles

April 5, 1994 _____

I dream that I take a shower and use a bottle of shampoo whose label reads: "Especially gentle for people with AIDS."

Through the shower doors, I see a grocery shelf filled with hundreds of these same bottles.

Stamped in large gray letters on every label are the words "It doesn't matter what it does. I'm going to die anyway."

Wish

_____

Henry, write me a prescription to remedy soul-weariness.

False Alarm

I sit in bed fully clothed and watch every in-and-out of Bill's chest. I fully expect that at any moment the bed will be soaked with his fluids, that everything inside him will come out. This is how I've heard death happens.

I look at his hands to see if they are the lobster claws of coma.

An hour ago we watched TV as usual and laughed over an *I Love Lucy* episode that we'd probably seen twenty times before. Ten o'clock came, and Bill aimed the remote and said something bizarre, something too bizarre to remember, something about the show *Picket Fences*, I think. It was a strange comment, garbled, senseless.

"What are you talking about?" I asked, my heart beating just a little faster.

Bill responded by telling me how much it had cost him to make photocopies the other day.

"What . . . ?" I said, thinking he must be having a stroke. He said something about the present we were making for Henry's fiftieth birthday, a miniature party scene with streamers and signs reading "Over the Hill."

"What's going on? What's the matter?" Panicked, I watched his eyes open, then close.

"Look at me," I said. "How many fingers am I holding up?"

"Two," he responded correctly.

"What day is today?"

"Friday."

"What holiday is coming up?"

"Memorial Day." His forehead felt cool.

He sat up and gave me the Beconase bottle so I could spray the ulcer on his tongue. He barely stayed awake long enough to open his mouth.

"I'm so tired," he said. "Remember that dream I told you about, the one I had last night about giving ten thousand dollars to the Lord's Pantry? It must have kept me up a couple of hours," he said. "That must be why I'm so tired."

That was the first I had heard about the dream. I knew he'd slept soundly last night.

He tried to put the Beconase back on the nightstand, but threw it on the floor instead.

"Leave it," I said.

"Don't you think he'll eat it?" Bill pointed to the dog.

I picked it up.

Bill must have realized something was wrong, that this fogginess around his brain and his words should not be, because he opened his nightstand drawer and found his blood pressure cuff. He fell asleep with the stethoscope in his ears.

"Let's go," I said, already out of my pajamas. I wanted to take him to the emergency room. Now.

He refused to go.

"Let me get some sleep," he said. "We'll see how I am in the morning."

Before he passed out, he said, "It looks like Henry will have to do that lumbar puncture." Henry has wanted to do a spinal tap on Bill for seven years now because of Bill's memory problems, his neurological complications. Bill has always refused.

I call Henry's answering service, but can't leave a message; he is out of town and the operator says he's not calling in. I don't believe her, but there is nothing I can do. I am near the phone; I will call an ambulance at the first sign of . . . well, anything.

Bill sleeps right now; he looks peaceful. I will wait until six-thirty before I try to wake him. Was it simply exhaustion that confused him, or a sudden physiological snap?

He breathes very deeply now. I have the light on, but Bill doesn't seem to notice. The dog is curled up behind Bill's knees, oblivious to these events.

I don't know what to do. Part of me, most of me, says to let him sleep through the night. Part of me wants to dial 911 and get him to the hospital. Part of me thinks I'm overreacting; one of Bill's last cogent sentences was "You've got to calm down."

He moved his legs and hands; this is good. He still breathes heavily but steadily. I try not to think of Alice and the deep, dark coma that preceded her death.

His stomach had hurt again today, after he'd felt pretty good for a couple of weeks. Henry had called in from Las Vegas and told Bill to go on a clear diet until he sees him Tuesday. Bill, who loves to eat so much, will have to go without food again. He has not eaten normally in months; he cramps with pain when even the smallest morsel of food hits his stomach.

We plan to go away on Wednesday, return to the place where we spent our honeymoon almost nine years ago. We went to the travel agent this afternoon and picked up our plane tickets; we're very excited. We last went to a travel agency in March; we planned to take a trip to Lourdes, a place of miracles. An hour after we left with our itinerary, Bill convulsed in the car and almost died. We canceled the trip, of course. Had Bill not gotten sick, we would have been in France this very evening.

He moved again, moistened his lips. He still breathes.

I don't feel as if I can go through another five weeks of Bill being in the hospital so soon after the five weeks he just spent there. Bill was admitted to the hospital after he collapsed in the car that day in March. He convulsed because he was in septic shock from infections racing through his abdomen. Infections like *Rhodococcus equii*, a bacterium usually confined to horses and discussed in veterinary journals. Bill had exploratory surgery during that hospitalization, and a nodule was removed from his ileum. Its removal did not end his pain, however. Now Bill, who under normal circumstances would gladly polish off a six-course meal, dares not eat anything more substantial than an ice pop or chicken broth.

It is so painful to watch. My strength is depleted; my hope is diminished. I will need other people to take charge for a while; I need somebody to adopt our dog. I cannot be responsible and thoughtful much longer.

I will not sleep tonight, despite the sleeping pill I took at nine-thirty, before Bill lost his mind.

"Bite your lips," I told him earlier today. "They have no color; they make me nervous."

Why are signs so oblique, and why can't I recognize trouble when it's in front of me? Bill left the apartment today with his fly open, but what man doesn't do that occasionally? After discovering his omission, Bill said, "Oh, God, we're going to have to start putting labels on things: teacup, refrigerator, dog." I laughed it off, said he has a lot on his mind, that it's okay to forget things sometimes. The other night he forgot to take off his glasses when he lay down to sleep.

What else, what else?

When he made the reservations for our trip last week, he kept confusing the dates. First he thought we'd arrive on Wednesday. Two minutes later he thought we'd arrive on Thursday; two more minutes, and it was Tuesday. I told him not to book anything until he felt more together. I thought he was just tired from studying for his financial planning exam, which he took last Saturday after pulling an all-nighter.

It is 12:01 A.M., and he still breathes.

For months, for years, I have refused to see in Bill the pattern I've seen in others with AIDS. The pattern of increasingly frequent hospitalizations. The chronicity of certain conditions: mouth ulcers, sinusitis, daily fevers that must be controlled with Naprosyn.

The dog just looked at me with sad, soulful eyes. His look said, "I know, I know. I'll stay next to him and keep him warm."

The need to always nap during the day, the moments of disorientation, his recent problem with bed-wetting, incontinence. These things don't happen to a healthy man, a man who is physically well. But I always remind Bill of his tremendous inner reserves. I always tell him: "Your five T cells are very efficient; they always pull you through." Wanting so badly to believe this myself, to make him believe it, to make him the exception to every AIDS rule.

Do others look at Bill and his pattern of sickness and say to themselves, as I've so often said about others, "It won't be long now"?

Oh, God. I wanted to give him a surprise party for his thirtieth birthday in November.

It is 12:17. Still breathing.

We haven't even lived in this apartment a year. Bill has

great plans to renovate the master bathroom and build a wood-paneled wall in the living room. When he feels a little better, he says.

The dog runs in his sleep; his body strains against the stillness of Bill.

Where is the pen Bill gave me for Christmas, the one my mother wrapped because he was in the hospital? I should write with that pen tonight, but I can't find it. I think it is out of ink anyway.

Wouldn't it be lovely if tomorrow morning Bill woke up perfectly lucid, able to think clearly about whether or not he should go to the hospital?

It is 12:26. He is on his back, with his right arm over his head, his hand in front of his eyes like a priest giving a blessing, or a person cringing in the face of a punishing blow.

Bill turns, and now I clearly see his face. It is full and round from the steroids he takes to keep inflammation at bay; his face does not look alarmingly pale. His lips tonight are slightly pink. Now his right arm curves gently over his head in an improvised ballet position. His lashes are long and dark on his cheeks, and I see the shadows of beard and mustache. Even when he's asleep, his hair remains perfectly in place.

I used to be able to sketch his face from memory, so defined are his features. How little they have changed in eleven years. No wrinkles, no lesions, no scars. His left hand clutches the comforter we share, and his wedding ring shines as if new.

It is 12:39, and I am tempted to think the rest of the night will go well, but I still fear what the morning will bring. I want to wake him, but this seems cruel. Let him rest; sleep is his only escape from himself these days. What are you dreaming, Bill? Are you deciding if you will return to me?

I beg you to return to me.

The sleeping pill makes my eyes water and my eyelids feel like stone, but I must stay awake. I know he is dying, know it with the same certainty I know my name. If I could orchestrate his death, plan it for him, I would make it quick, make it happen before he witnesses his own deterioration. Yes, I want him to die quickly, but no, I don't want him to die yet.

I want just a little more time with him.

It is such a waste; it is the world's loss. The nuns used to say that God takes special people early because he can't bear to be parted from them.

What about those of us who are left behind when you take them, God? We can't bear to be parted from them either.

I do not want to sleep; I do not want to dream. I fear my dreams as much as I fear my awakening. My dreams have been grotesque, surreal, lately, filled with disjointed images: throwing cheese sandwiches in a gymnasium, dancing an erotic tango with a priest.

Who can help me tonight? I used to pray that the Blessed Mother would appear to me in a dream; I prayed for her to soothe me. Once, when I was six years old and in my grandmother's bed with fever, I looked at a statue of the Virgin, and, right before my eyes, it slid from one end of the bureau to the other. I told my mother and my grandmother, but they obviously thought me delirious. I'm not so sure; I can still hear the scraping sound of plaster against glass.

I pray for that sound again, for the comfort of company. I pray for her to visit; she doesn't even have to wait for a dream. I pray for her to save Bill's life.

It is 1:10 and he still breathes, the dog still sleeps, and I grow more and more weary.

It is Memorial Day weekend. Who will I remember? I will remember Jack and Meg and Timothy and Mark and Barbara and Danny and Harry and Elizabeth and Alice. Who else? We have all fought, and most of us have died in the battle, our defenses decimated. I look at Bill and the truth is unavoidable; it is as if I already remember him as a person who was, not as a person who lives and lies beside me tonight. It is Bill I will remember this Memorial Day, the next Memorial Day, for as many Memorial Days as I survive.

It is on Bill's grave that I will weep.

It is no use. I must sleep, but I will sleep with my hearing aids in and my clothes on. I will sleep touching Bill, if indeed I sleep at all.

Good night, my love.

May 28, 1994 _____

The loveliness occurred. Bill woke up coherent, rested, and without a clue as to what happened last night; he doesn't remember a thing. Not the blood pressure cuff, not the rambling comments, not even his brief conversation with his mother at nine forty-five. When I told him what happened, he said he'd better take his temperature. With the thermometer in his mouth, he looked at his nightstand and handed me two bottles: imipramine and temazepam. An antidepressant and a sleeping pill. He had never taken them together before last night. Both are sedatives on their own. Are they a super-sedative when combined?

So it appears his delirium was nothing more than the temporary effects of an overdose.

Smiling, he said he had a wonderful sleep.

Tenacity

On June 17, I landed in the hospital with the condition I most feared: CMV retinitis. Unlike Bill, my CMV manifested itself visually in the form of dark spots and lines in front of my eyes.

Bill, hospitalized continuously now since the first of June, had lasted only a few vacation hours before his small intestine ruptured. He was now on the fifth floor of our Yonkers hospital; I was on the seventh. Hospital regulations forbid us from sharing a room, and Henry did not even want us on the same floor, fearing that our medicines would get mixed up.

For years, Henry had called us "Ping and Pong" because we so conveniently took turns getting sick.

In June, we lost that nickname, and crashed right into each other.

The day your intestine finally exploded, after months of doubling you over with pain, after months of eluding the tests that looked in you and through you, after months of building up to its final rupture, I looked out the windowed wall of our hotel room and saw the same trees and mountains I had first seen on our honeymoon nine years ago. Now rain obscured my view, kept me from seeing beyond the walls of this place, made me disbelieve that another place could exist, or ever existed. But nine years ago the mountains had burst with the prismatical glory of autumn, with leaves that, in the very moment before their final fall to earth, were at their most beautiful.

On this night I could do nothing but pick up the phone and say "Help me."

I could not say that you excused yourself from the dining room soon after we sat down, and never returned. I could not say that you literally crawled from the public rest room to our private room and phoned the front desk before you collapsed. I could not say that you were now knotted up on our bed, face smeared with tears and sweat, groans tearing from your throat as your insides tore themselves apart.

I could say none of these things. I could only say "Help."

Into your abdomen roared fluid and bile and infection, a whirlpool that devoured and digested the very life of you. You cried years of tears, and I helplessly witnessed your pain, lancing pain, pain that reached its hand inside you and pulled so intently that you must have thought God wrenched out your very soul.

Medics arrived soon after my call. They gently unknotted you and wheeled you out the same door you had entered only five hours earlier, past the line of guests straining to see the reason for their shattered peace.

I drove on winding, unlit roads, desperately trying to follow you in your ambulance, but I lost you around the first curve; you went too fast. My eyes felt dry and lifeless, and strange lights and lines marred my vision. I no longer felt able to respond to crises; instead of an expected rush of adrenaline—you needed me, after all—I felt the stupefaction of surrender. You had fallen; you, the person I never believed would fall.

First you went to a local hospital, but were quickly rerouted to a larger facility. Again I followed your ambulance in our rental car; again I lost you. I fought the forces of gravity and sleep, fought the impulse to simply close my eyes and keep them shut on this lonely road. They ached and compelled me to drive more slowly, to lose you so quickly in the midnight rain.

The doctors at the second hospital thrust tubes and catheters and fingers at you and into you. The examining room seemed too bright; it was shiny and steely and foillike, a place in which to wrap you up and store you until a later time. The next morning you finally closed your morphine-laden eyelids, and I collapsed into a chair by your bed and slept for an hour as if anesthetized, reluctantly tearing my gaze away from your bluish face.

Then, so quickly, to surgery. You were almost in the operating room when a nurse looked down and said, "This will have to go," and handed me your wedding ring. You were already unconscious from pain. I was exquisitely conscious of my own.

An hour later the surgeon emerged. You were still on the table, he said, and he had cut away eleven inches of hole-ridden bowel; he had taken your stoma to the surface to save it. You were his first HIV surgical patient; he was a resident in training. Perhaps his inexperience made him arrogant, made him look at me as if only he had the inside story, made him stare me down without a visible trace of compassion and let me know that he held your life in his hands, and I didn't.

He didn't look like God to me.

The doctor acted as if you were just another case, and a pathetic one at that, and that is probably what you were. He said your condition was invariably fatal, that he would close you up but he didn't expect you to live. I thought of you lying on the operating table while medical students practiced on you, tried to make you fit into the textbooks they'd read.

For eight years I have known you are not a textbook case, that nothing about you is open-and-shut.

My heart tore away his complacency, screamed that he only knew your numbers, not you. How dare he write you off? But shock quieted me, and I simply nodded and cursed him silently. I watched him reenter the surgical suite and hated the thought that he would touch you again.

But somehow you got off that table, and I saw you later that night, unconscious. One machine breathed for you, another handled your digestion. Machines crowded that tiny cell and lived for you, but I didn't care.

It was the living that mattered.

Will I ever forget your terror when you woke and found yourself strapped to devices, felt your immobility and your inability to speak? At that moment of your awakening I wanted nothing more than to pour myself into your body, enter it through the perforations in your bowel, slide away with you to darkness, or somehow take the darkness into myself and leave behind only light.

One by one the tubes came out, and you were transferred by ambulance to our hospital in Yonkers as soon as it seemed that you might not die on the trip home. The New England doctors wanted you gone; you were too high-risk. It would have been easier for them had you died, had you slid neatly into a preconceived slot, tagged and forgotten once the door finally closed. But you lived, and they didn't know if they could keep you alive.

At first I thought they wanted you gone because you haunted them. I see now that they weren't haunted by you at all; they probably didn't even think much about you.

I am haunted by them and their indifference.

Because you were supposed to die, you weren't given the

drains routinely inserted to siphon away fluids that sit and fester and infect. So you underwent another surgery in New York to put in the drains, but it was too late. Your belly swelled like a pregnant woman's womb until you no longer had any blood pressure and your body started cooling with death instead of heating up with the fever of life.

That was the worst night, when I looked at you and you were so close to leaving, when I waited with your mother outside your closed door for two, maybe three hours, not knowing if you still breathed. At seven forty-one a chill went down my spine. I looked at the reflection of the setting sun in the windows and thought you had died. But you hadn't. It was just a chill.

We bartered for time; you needed more surgery but also needed a day to stabilize after being revived. You held steady. When, forty-eight hours later, our surgeon opened you up for the third time in three weeks, he found a dime-sized hole at the point of resection, a place that had been closed with stitches intended for a corpse, not for a person who might rise and walk again.

Your stomach is quiet now. It still hurts, but hurting has become the norm, not the exception. We hope it is merely incisional pain, not a slow-burning fuse waiting until we become complacent before it fully reignites. A bag now catches and discards what your small intestine once caught and absorbed. We do not know what made your intestine explode in the first place. We do not know if it will explode again.

You are ninety-eight pounds now and starving; you have not eaten for weeks and have been kept alive with total parenteral nutrition. But you walked today, shuffled really, hunched over your IV pole like an eighty-year-old man at the end of his days instead of a twenty-nine-year-old who should not be nearing his.

But I am nonetheless grateful for these minor miracles: a shuffle here, a smile there.

I gazed at you so intently this afternoon that you asked me what was wrong. You cannot yet comprehend, or perhaps do not yet believe, that I am watching you die, that I can hold you as tightly as I can and protect you from some of the dangers outside but cannot protect you from your combative world within. You cannot comprehend that I need to memorize every movement of your eyelids, every nuance of color of your skin, every passage of your tongue over cracked and waterless lips. I need to memorize all of these before my eyes fail me, and your face, like our life together, becomes only a memory.

I need to see the ring back on your finger and know it is still the same ring that shone so brightly nine years ago. I need to know it is the same ring that once promised hope, and still does.

I need to watch the leaves of our life fall and finally blow away with the winds of the season.

I need to watch them and remember how beautiful their colors once were.

Free Fall

I can no longer remember what happened when; the last seventy-nine days blur into a single prolonged nightmare.

What started on the first of June is still unfolding. What started almost nine years ago is about to end.

You have had five surgeries so far to fix an intestine that won't stop destroying itself, that won't stop eating holes in its walls like moths in a sweater. I can't remember most of the details of the prior surgeries. I tick them off as they occur: one, two, three, four, five. The last surgery showed a hole the diameter of a tennis ball, a hole that caused more fetid fluid to flood your abdomen, to catch your innards and twist them and paste them together in a way nature never intended.

You were not expected to survive this surgery, just as you were not expected to survive the four preceding it. But you did, and I don't know if that is good or bad. After the last surgery, we had to wait until 11:00 P.M. to see you, when the recovery room nurse snuck us in. You woke up and recognized me—how grateful I was—and you breathed on your own, no ventilator. You asked me if the surgeon was happy, and I said yes, because he was, at the time, and you fell back to sleep. And although you slept, you talked and moved and opened your eyes and told me you had to stack the quarters you imagined you saw on your blankets, the coins you normally stacked on your dresser at home every night before going to bed.

This is the sequence of events: On the first of June you were hospitalized during our short-lived trip to New England and were later moved to our Yonkers hospital. You remained there until August sixth, when you were discharged. You were back in the hospital on the tenth, readmitted after being home for barely five days. Those five days showed us how little was left of you, how far you had fallen.

When you came home for those few days, you sat on the couch where Pug had lain at your side before we had to give him up—a fifteen-pound dog had become too much work. You sat frustrated and leashed to the end of your IV pole; you could no longer eat. You remembered the joy of chewing a steak, of drinking a glass of wine, but these were luxuries no longer allowed. While you were home I took my food and walked around the apartment with it, to the office, to the bedroom, to the hallway, to any place other than the living room where you sat.

I could not witness your hunger and longing for the things I could still do.

I took your blood pressure. I recorded your temperature and your urine output. I drew up syringes of Demerol and shot it into your meatless buttocks or injected it into a bag that dripped into a vein. Three nights after you came home, you shook ceaselessly in our bed while you slept, trembling, moving, gyrating every muscle and nerve when you should have been resting, doing all the living you wanted to do while asleep that you could no longer do while awake.

On the morning of the fifth day, you were feverish and weak. I watched you try to get your precious spoon of ice to your mouth, and it was as if you were trying to balance it over many miles, or up and down steep mountains; that is how shaky you were. Slowly you moved the spoon toward your mouth and positioned it carefully, your forehead clammy with the effort. Then you thrust the spoon toward your lips and spilled most of the ice; you saved only a few slivers.

You were readmitted that day. Henry knew in his heart how sick you were; he knew, perhaps, that you shouldn't have been discharged at all. But he also knew that your sanity depended on a few days' reprieve. You cried when he told you to go back to the hospital.

You said, "I won't survive another surgery. But what choice do I have?"

I said then the hardest words I will ever have to say in my life.

"Our life as we know it is over. It will never be the same again."

You cried a little more, then nodded and unhooked yourself from your IV for just a short time and walked around the apartment slowly, unused to moving so freely, so unencumbered. You sat on the terrace that you had little chance to enjoy, because you've been so sick since we moved into this apartment last year. You just sat there and said, "But it's such a beautiful day."

And it was, almost like spring in the middle of August. I turned my head and went inside. I knew this was the last time you would sit on our terrace. I knew you were saying good-bye, and I couldn't bear to hear the words.

I packed your bag with fewer things than I'd ever packed for you before. I placed them in the bag we had bought especially for our vacation because its wheels made it easier to transport. You grabbed the bag despite your weakness and walked out of our building with your back straight and your steps firm. You went to the driver's side of our car, not to drive, but to open the door for me, as if this were our first date, as if you were saying you would take care of me for as long as you could, in whatever way you could.

We hadn't even gone a block when you said, "Tell me right now if you think I'm crazy to go back in again. Just say the word, and I'll go home with you and never go back."

I said, as I kept driving, "No, you're not crazy. Everything is out of our hands now."

You were in your hospital room five minutes when a nurse ushered me down the hall to the kitchen. You had lost your blood pressure again, the second time in two months. I saw the crash cart burst into your room, followed by Henry. I tried to run after them both, but the nurses held me back. They streamed in and out of the kitchen where I sat; they positioned themselves in the doorway so I could not see beyond it.

They revived you, and Henry was behind that, of course, always there when you crashed, always giving you a hand up when you fell.

You went to the ICU, and Henry did more tests and found more holes in your bowel. He said he must operate again, and you looked at me wordlessly, but I swear you pleaded: Can't you stop this from happening.

I told you we would follow your wishes, no matter what they were.

"What choice do I have?" you said once again, and gave the go-ahead for the operation.

You agreed to do what needed to be done, but I think you sanctioned something more. I think you agreed to die.

You survived that last operation. Your mother and I sat with you the next day, although you remained unconscious through most of it. But you continued your pantomime of life while you slept. You pretended to put food in your mouth; you pointed to places and things as if conducting a class. You pretended to type and drive, and you talked nonsense in your sleep, with a wonderful vocabulary.

The morning after this surgery you talked to your IV pole, thinking in your confusion it was me, and became angry when it didn't respond. The nurse thought you prayed when she heard your solitary voice, but she intervened when you started to yell.

"I'm talking to Janice!" you barked.

You then woke up a bit and saw that what you thought was my hair was actually your yellow bag of nutrition. You went in and out of consciousness that day. You told us you floated above your body; you viewed us from a strange perspective somewhere above your bed. You were not frightened, though; you were fascinated.

For a while you forgot you could talk, and gestured for paper and pen.

You wrote: "I dreamed I saw that the expiration date on the jar of Tabasco sauce was 3/31/79."

"What do you think that means?" I asked.

"I don't know what it means," you said. "It's just what I saw."

A little later you wrote: "Water cup and green swab stick, SVP."

"Please," you wrote in French. Relieve my thirst.

This time you didn't recover as you always had before, in the way that made people shake their heads in disbelief. Your ostomy never really woke up; you poured blood from your incision; you sprouted new and dangerous infections. You related a nightmare: Henry, a professor, was giving out assignments to students lined up in front of him.

"I looked at my assignment and knew I wasn't up to the task he gave me," you said.

I never thought to ask you about the other students. Were they Henry's living patients, or were you beside Alice and Danny?

Was I there?

I related this dream to Henry, and he sadly patted your leg.

"You will always be able to meet any task I give you," he told you.

It is already a week after surgery, yet you still sleep more than you do not, you still pantomime life while you dream. You make little affectionate gestures to me when you do wake—a nose tweak, a face touch.

Once while you slept, I whispered in your ear, "Go, if you need to go."

Eyes closed, you nodded, and I thought that perhaps you would.

Instead, you opened your eyes and said, "But I wanted to see a picture of Puggy first," before falling back to sleep and not dying.

When I left you today, you looked fairly good, if tired, and after consulting the TV listings said you'd call between eight and ten o'clock tonight. Which you didn't. So I waited until ten, hoping that you just waited for a show to end, hoping that you remembered who I was and why you should call me, but ten o'clock came and went, and so I called you. Delirious, you whispered that you had fever, and pain, that the nurses were there and you couldn't stay on the phone.

"I'll talk to you later," you said.

I hung up and realized I'd forgotten to say "I love you."

Your temperature is 103; the fever and the sickness and the painkillers—Demerol every two hours, Dilaudid injections in between—confuse you.

"Do you have my number?" I asked the nurse I called as soon as I hung up with you.

Yes, she did.

"Should I call you if something bad happens?" she asked.

It was the first time anyone had asked me that question and seemed to mean it. Before this night I had counted on your incredible resilience; I'd assumed that, no matter how bad it got, you would later tell me how it felt. But this night my assumptions crumbled. It was the first time I thought something bad might really happen.

There is no longer any question in my mind: I am losing you. I walk the apartment in the dark hours of the morning because I have forgotten how to sleep, how to rest, how to do human things.

I thirst for you, but I, too, can no longer drink.

Gone

And so it has happened. After all of the days and nights and years of thinking that somehow you would be the first to outwit this disease, of thinking that you, of all people, would somehow be stronger.

You are gone.

It happened only days after I asked God for a sign to guide me. I walked the halls of our apartment one night and prayed and agonized over the meaning of your suffering. When I woke up the next morning, I discovered that one of your angelfish had died overnight. I decided to stop asking God for signs.

On Saturday morning, the twentieth of August, I called your room, knowing you wouldn't answer, driven to try anyway. The phone rang six, seven, eight times. Then someone picked up the receiver and broke the connection. The phone was busy when I tried again.

Henry had picked up the phone and left it off the hook. He called me at eleven that morning and spoke quietly and intensely; I had no trouble hearing him.

"I am beginning to doubt Bill's viability," he said.

He said these words as facts, and I believed them as such.

"Please come over to see him. Now."

Your parents were already on their way to our place; they wanted us to go to the hospital together. But I couldn't wait, so I gathered some pictures that spanned the time of our beginning to the time of our end, and threw some of our old love letters into a bag. I wrote a note to your parents: "Henry called. I'm at the hospital. It is bad."

It was long before normal visiting hours, but you weren't surprised to see me. You were in bed, of course. For so many days now you had been in bed, too weak to get up, in too much pain to move. You were unshaven but clean; you spit toothpaste water into a kidney-shaped bowl as I walked in. You smiled, as always, and I perched on the edge of the bed, as always.

"How are you?" I asked, and you gave your usual response.

"I'm fine."

I took out the pictures and taped a big black-and-white photo of us to the wall where you could see it without trying too hard, the photo where we lay on pillows with our arms around each other. It was taken a lifetime ago; it was taken last year.

I showed you the other photographs. Two were from 1984: Sacre Coeur, our flat in London. Our wedding picture and a picture of Puggy. A picture of Henry's office, a picture of our kitchen taken after you renovated it last summer. You looked at each one as I explained them, and I was afraid I'd insulted you, but I was also afraid that I really needed to explain them.

Then I read a few of the letters. We laughed at the people

we once were; we couldn't believe such people ever existed. Your parents arrived. Then your sister and brother, then my parents, until finally you asked me to have everyone leave for a while; it was all too much.

"What's going on?" you asked when they left.

"You're very sick" was all I managed.

"I'm very sick," you repeated, and then you put it all together: why I was there so early, why everyone else was so anxious to see you.

Before I even reached your room that morning, a nurse asked if I would agree to put you on morphine. They could no longer ask you these kinds of questions, I suppose, or perhaps they could ask them but no longer rely upon your answers.

"Do whatever it takes," I said, knowing that morphine made you strange and confused, but also knowing it was the only thing that could keep you from the pain that increased with each passing minute. You needed a huge induction dose: you were so used to painkillers that it would take a tremendous amount of morphine to place you in the desired state.

And I suppose, in truth, that the desired state at this point was coma, then death.

When I entered your room, I noticed that no bags of antibiotics hung from your IV pole; they could no longer help you. I don't think you noticed this, but your body did: it burned with fevers reaching 105 degrees. I swabbed your brow, and you didn't fight me, although you always had been phobic about the feeling of water on your face.

Henry came in, and you didn't seem to be there, so we talked as if you weren't. I mentioned that you had been speaking gibberish earlier.

Then you woke up for a moment and said, with perfect clarity, "I'm not making any sense?"

Henry said it was okay, that sometimes he didn't make

any sense either. He then turned to me and said, "You'll stay here tonight."

I saw panic in your eyes, but you held yourself together, as always; you didn't make a scene or act in any way uncontrolled. You looked to Henry for an explanation; he told you I could be trusted to keep you out of pain. The explanation satisfied you, and you looked at Henry then, and you smiled. Words, for that moment and for most of the moments thereafter, were beyond you. You could do nothing but reach for his hand.

Then you opened your arms, and the two of you embraced and gazed at each other; a veritable lifetime of shared work passed between you.

I stayed with you that night, and you told me you didn't want your morphine increased; you didn't want to be crazy for your last hours. But our need to be merciful made us make you crazy, and your pain was so bad that the nurses didn't even wait for my instructions. They had their own instructions from Henry, and these were to keep you pain-free. You received more and more morphine, until I thought that you must die, if only from an overdose.

But you didn't. In fact, you never slept that night. You had moments of lucidity interspersed with longer moments of strange ramblings. You tried to pull out your nasogastric tube; I stopped you. Then I saw blood on your sheets, and yelled for the nurse. You told me to stop worrying so much.

"I'll be fine," you said.

But the nurse discovered that you had pulled out your IV and she explained this as she inserted a new line. You turned to me with arms outstretched and cried: "Oh, thank you, Thank you!" and I told you I would protect you, that nobody would ever look out for you the way I would.

You touched my hair and whispered, "I know."

I lay down on a cot, but never slept. About once an hour you regained consciousness and looked around the room for

ne and waited for me to say, "I'm here." Then you opened
your arms and held me, crying sometimes, stroking me, kiss-
ng me passionately and tenderly.

Once, you moved your fingers through my hair in the
same gesture you had used when we made love. I think you
were making love to me for the last time that night.

I know it was beautiful.

At two or three in the morning you motioned for me to
come closer.

"Would you mind if I died?" you said, nodding, as if you
had just made a decision. "Because I think I'm going to die
from this. But I'd like it to be after the operation on Monday."

You referred to the only remaining thing that could be
done for you: the entire removal of your small intestine.
Henry had mentioned the possibility as something we could
consider after the weekend. You held on to that thread of
hope, even while acknowledging that you would never survive it. I wonder if I would have given permission for the
surgery had Monday come and you still lived. I will never
know; you spared me that decision by dying before I had to
make it.

Throughout the night, from Saturday to Sunday, you babbled and gestured and intermittently woke up. Once you admired the cross you had given me for my birthday so many
years before, and I asked if you wanted it around your neck.
You nodded. A little later you woke and saw my engagement
ring. You studied it at length, took it off my finger, and tried
to put it on your own. It wouldn't fit; your hands had bal-
looned from sepsis.

You found words again, briefly.

"It's the most beautiful thing I've ever seen."

I told you the story of your going to Philadelphia to buy it
for me, as if you had never heard the tale before and had certainly not lived it. Finally you gave the ring back.

"Now you can do whatever you want," you said.

"Don't be silly," I replied. "I'm putting it right back on my finger." And that's what I did.

You spoke the strange language of the dying that night, so oddly beautiful to hear. It was a language of one-syllable words ending in "sh." I tried to decipher your meaning.

"Brush? Do you want me to brush your hair?" I'd say, desperate to communicate with the person I always could communicate with wordlessly. I kept asking the question until you finally realized I was no longer speaking the same language as you, and you sighed, remembered English for a phrase, and said, "Okay."

Relieved, knowing you humored me, I brushed your hair. At times, variations on this sound escaped your lips—*fresh? wish? fish?*—exhalations of breath after a long journey, psalms praising the God you approached.

When the shift changed in the morning, you realized that had never met one of the nurses now standing by your bed. With all of your innate graciousness intact, you introduced us. I laughed, because you were still so charming and concerned about me.

Then you told the nurse, "Marrying Janice was the smartest thing I ever did in my life."

Those were the last words I ever heard you speak.

Henry came in around noon, when you were having a seizure. You still hadn't slept; agitated, you fought for every second of life. Henry watched, then made the gesture I had so long dreaded: he motioned for me to come outside. Your mother, who had joined us by that time, gasped just a little before she turned her attention back to you.

We sat in the solarium outside your room, and Henry didn't waste words.

"Bill is dying," he said.

I felt as crazed and incoherent as you must have felt on morphine, as if I no longer had control of my own thoughts.

Henry held my hand; there was very little to say. When we returned, he gave you a shot of phenobarbital to calm the seizures.

"Your job now is to relax, Bill," he said.

He only returned once more before you died. By two o'clock on Sunday afternoon, you had lapsed into your final coma.

Your brother and sister came that afternoon, as did your parents and my parents. My sister and her husband drove down from Boston; my brother came from Connecticut. At about three o'clock I sat on the cot, our mothers on either side of me, and cried, a horrible, violent crying, loud, tearing, unlike any crying I've done before or since.

"He's dying; God, he's dying!" I sobbed.

I don't know if you heard me, but I think you did, because at that moment you had your first death convulsion. You seized and gasped for breath, your eyes unseeing pinpoints of morphine.

"He's going!" I cried, and ran to the bed.

I told the nurses it was your time, and they believed me, and brought me a chair. But although your time had started, it was far from over. Almost every hour you had a seizure that lasted about twenty minutes, each one a little more agonizing than the one before it. I heard the others cry; I heard them try to soothe each other. But it was as if their voices were muted, as if they were talking in another country. The only voice I heard clearly was yours.

Your mother and I stayed with you the entire night. The house doctor gave you a Valium push to calm you, although it was unusual for a person on so much morphine to need even more sedation. I never knew dying would be so hard, but it was. Around three in the morning I heard the death rattle in your chest. Morphine relaxes the lungs, and you were dying from pneumonia. I told you to stop breathing, to focus your eyes on me and die, that it would be safe for you to go

as long as you looked at me, and we did lock eyes, although
it is hard for me to believe you actually saw me.

By six-fifteen Monday morning you still hadn't died. I
leaned over to you and said, "Your mother and I are going
into the solarium for a little while, if you want to die by
yourself."

Not even ten minutes had passed when a nurse motioned
us to return. There you were, your eyes slightly open, your
chest still, lying in that same interchangeable bed in the same
interchangeable room you had been in probably a dozen
times before; the only difference was that this time you
would not leave by your own power. So kind you were even
in death; you spared us the torture of seeing you take your
last breath.

Your mother and I held each other and cried. Then she
closed your eyes and said, "You've seen enough, William."

I took the cross from your neck and put it back on my
own. Then we left so the nurse could clean you, and when
we next saw you, your tubes and IVs and bags were all gone,
and it was just you again, beautiful, handsome, whole. We
packed up your belongings: the picture I had taped to the
wall the previous day, your toothbrush, your slippers, stained
from the medicine and blood and infection of the last two
months. I kissed you while your lips were still warm, and
rolled our special vacation bag down the hall.

Henry called and asked to speak with me. I could barely
hear him; I think I wished my ears could close like your
eyes.

"How are you?" Henry asked, his voice cracking.

I don't remember what I said, but I handed the phone to
your mother. I signed the release for your autopsy.

It poured rain outside, and the storm only got worse as the
day progressed, with hurricanelike winds and flooding grave
violence. I think the world cried that day. Henry called me
later with your autopsy results: internal bleeding, sepsis

leaks throughout your abdomen. I already knew this; during that last day I had smelled your dying with your every outward breath. Dying smells like vase water after the flowers have been removed—oversweet, stinging. After you died, you no longer had that smell, and I felt relieved.

We had your services near your hometown, as you wanted, and at least two hundred people attended. On Wednesday night I sat by your casket; I looked up and saw Henry kneeling by your side. He prayed a long time, then turned to me with tears running down his cheeks.

"Doctors aren't supposed to be emotional," he said, and then we just stood with our arms around each other.

He asked you questions: Why was your vision never affected by your CMV? Why couldn't he stop the ulcerative process that killed you?

Family members approached and thanked Henry, and about an hour later I left to walk him to his car. But when we got outside, he pointed to a bench, and we sat for another half hour together, talking, questioning, disbelieving, until my father told us it was already ten o'clock, that we had to say good night to you.

We went back inside, and Henry leaned over your casket and kissed you good-bye. It was then I noticed that your hair had gone gray at the temples. It must have happened that last week, perhaps even that last day.

You are buried with your great-great-grandparents, two grandmothers, and two cousins in a family plot. I visited you this past weekend and saw that the big mound of dirt covering you since the twenty-sixth of August had flattened a bit. Your nieces visited you before I did, and had artfully rearranged the flowers on your grave.

In pebbles, they had spelled out a message.

"Love you."

Eulogy

I delivered the following eulogy at a memorial service for Bill on September 28, 1994, at Graymoor Christian Unity Center in Garrison, New York. Bill and I met many of the people mentioned in this book through an HIV support group held there each Saturday: Meg, Timothy, Harry, Danny, Mark, Elizabeth, Barbara, Alice. Graymoor is the monastery with the large roadside crucifix that I passed on the day of my car accident.

About fifty people attended Bill's service, and most of them were AIDS activists, people touched by Bill's courage and willingness to go public with his life, with his message. After a number of musical selections, readings, and reflections, I delivered the eulogy I had often prayed I wouldn't have to deliver.

I've rewritten this eulogy about five times, and I am still dissatisfied. Nothing I say seems to capture Bill's uniqueness, his personality, his quirkiness. Each revision was reduced to just a list of generalities and grand themes: Bill the dedicated volunteer, Bill the long-term survivor, Bill the fighter. All of these characterizations are true, but none provide a complete picture.

Bill was a man who lived and died with AIDS, but this is not the only way, or the primary way, he should be described. By remembering Bill only as a person with AIDS, I would be, in effect, doing the very thing he most despised. I would be creating a caricature of a person with AIDS, complete with all of the appropriate adjectives, and calling it Bill. Bill was certainly a character, but he was certainly not a caricature.

My husband of almost nine years, the love of my life for eleven, was a brilliant, witty man. I met him when he was just eighteen years old. He grinned at me, and I'm sure he held out his hand for me to shake, because that was the polite thing to do, and then he introduced himself as the center for Villanova's basketball team. This was vintage Bill: revealing himself with all of his perceived imperfections right away, so that we wouldn't have to waste time worrying about them later. This is much the same way he approached the disclosure of his HIV status. He simply told people he was positive, let them see that he was a whole person first, and a person with a disease second, and then got on with the task at hand, which was living.

Bill was an intellectual who never took himself too seriously. A straight-A student, he graduated magna cum laude from Villanova University in 1985. He started graduate school and received his M.B.A. years after he was diagnosed with HIV.

Bill had many loves in life. He adored anything high-tech and on the cutting edge: he was always upgrading our computer, audio equipment, televisions. When a new electronic hearing aid came on the market, he insisted I be upgraded, too.

He loved to spend money on good clothes, vacations spent in the finest hotels, meals in the best restaurants. He loved working with his hands, and was an excellent carpenter, with the ability to design and build just about anything he envisioned. Although it seems a lifetime away, it was only a year ago that he completely renovated our kitchen, building new cabinets, tiling the walls and floor, installing new countertops. He loved tending to his two fish tanks and often stayed up until the early hours of the morning nursing sick fish or catching babies in a special compartment to keep them from being eaten. He loved our dog, Puggy, whom he called "son" in a baby voice that was so unlike his normal speech.

He loved the people society rejected, and spent many hours in college volunteering at a school for handicapped children. It was grueling, strenuous work, and he loved it so much that he took night classes to accommodate it. He loved his career as a computer consultant; he loved his later career as an activist. He loved his family and my family; he loved his friends and colleagues. He loved the nurses who cared for him over the years, and he loved the doctor who was so devoted to him and cherished him.

And he loved me, a miracle for which I will never stop thanking God.

There's so much more to be said about Bill: that his friends said that every hair on his head was numbered and jumped into place at his command. That he had a photographic memory for anything mathematical and knew all of his credit card numbers by heart. That his idea of exercise was to sit at his computer and type. That, at last count, he belonged to more than thirty-five frequent flier programs and knew the three-letter abbreviation for every airport in the United States. That he loved to eat exotic food—antelope, turtle, snake—and made the best cheesecake I ever tasted. That he thought calculus was fun. That he liked the music of the Talking Heads, the B52s, *Les Miserables*, and *The Rocky*

Horror Picture Show. That he absolutely hated to dance and couldn't ski or roller-skate to save his life.

These are pieces of Bill that hardly touch upon his essence, his core. And if I were to summarize his essence, in a word, I would have to choose the word "love." Because love was so integral to Bill, having a love relationship with him was easy and never involved any elaborate head games or jealousies. Love was simple to Bill, and here was his creed: If you love someone, you share your love with that person no matter who it is, and don't worry about appearances, rules, or implications.

I cannot relate all of the anecdotes of our lifetime together, but I will save them for another time, to allow us to savor Bill frequently and fondly in the future.

But I would like to tell you a story that began during the last days of Bill's life and ended a week after his death. It is a story that had made me question my own sanity from time to time, but which has never ceased to comfort me. I hope you will also find comfort in hearing it.

A few nights before Bill died, I couldn't sleep, and stayed up asking God for a sign to help me understand what was painfully unfolding in his hospital room. When I woke up the next day, I discovered that one of Bill's beloved angelfish had died overnight. Three angelfish remained in the tank. I cursed God for choosing such a lousy sign, yet that angelfish clarified what I had been denying for months: that Bill's time was running out and that his death was imminent.

And indeed, Bill began dying within hours of this discovery.

Two nights before he died, during his last hours of lucidity, Bill asked me if I minded if he died. During these final hours of consciousness, he let down his carefully constructed proprieties and sang me the most beautiful love song I've ever heard, its notes transcending the tubes and pumps and IVs that chained him to his bed. His last words were not about regret or disappointment or anger; his last words during the early morning hours between Saturday and Sunday were about our love for each other. He was again the wonderfully vulnerable boy I had first met in 1983; here was the spontaneous Bill, the unencumbered Bill, the romantic Bill.

His words and embraces were so complete and so magical that I think perhaps it was the finest night of our marriage.

A week later I returned home after Bill's funeral, accompanied by my sister and her family. We sat up for a while and reminisced and wished that somehow Bill could give us a sign to let us know that he was all right. Before going to bed, I walked over to the angelfish tank and stopped dead in my tracks.

Four angelfish now swam where there had only been three.

I asked my family to count them, thinking I hallucinated, and their answers were all the same: four angelfish now lived in these waters.

Alone on the left side of the tank, separated from the other three fish, swam a pearl-colored angelfish that resembled the one I had discarded days earlier. I realized then that I had received the comforting sign I so desired, a sign that counteracted the jarring death of the angelfish a week earlier. A sign, I felt, that showed me that perhaps death is not so final after all.

I watched this beautiful fish for a long time, and he looked right back at me, or so I imagined. And then it became clear that this little one was, in its own way, asking me to do what Bill had asked me to do eleven years earlier: to listen to the call of the heart and swim with him in the waters of love. Eleven years ago I gladly jumped in; I could do no less that night.

And so I trusted the love that washed over me in such an unexpected form. I suspended cynicism and dove again into the waters that defined Bill, water so clear you could see straight to the bottom and witness all the colors and joys of life teeming above and below its surface.

Bill flowed with the currents of his life and situation and was brought to undreamed-of depths. Of the two of us, he was the stronger swimmer, and he allowed me to hold on to his powerful back while, stroke after stroke, year after year, he delved first into uncharted waters. He was the first to have the HIV test and the first to learn its results; he showed me how to approach my own test and how to react to whatever the verdict might be. He had an AIDS diagnosis before I did and showed me how even a queasy person could live with a Portacath and administer his own IV antibiotics.

He showed me how to do these things before my own time came to do them. He witnessed the deterioration of his body and yet showed me it was possible to still live gracefully, productively, and with tremendous dignity.

He showed me how to die.

I gazed into the tank that night and was flooded with Bill's presence. At that moment I understood that what happened to Bill had to happen, that there is a movement to the waters of life that we cannot always discern and certainly cannot control, that we must allow ourselves to be drawn to wherever the tide takes us. At that moment I knew Bill was at peace, and although I feel I will never stop mourning for him, I have stopped fearing for him.

I knew in my heart that this angelfish would not be with us for long, that something so precious must return to its source. And indeed, twenty-four hours later, my little angelfish began to die. He stopped eating; he developed a gruesome eye infection. Blind and dying, he staggered around his world, banged into the walls, lost his balance while he swam. His suffering was so great, so unbearable to watch, that we did the only thing that could be done; we euthanized him and said our good-byes and were left to contemplate a strange and unexplainable event in the form of an angelfish that lived, suffered, and died with such tremendous meaning.

Bill taught me the greatest lessons of life simply by living his own: that to be allowed to swim in the waters of love you must be prepared to sometime wash onto the shores of suffering. That a lifetime spent treading water and never diving below its surface is a life unfulfilled.

Although I have come to peace with Bill's death, there is still not a day, an hour, or a minute that I do not miss him. I can't imagine a future day, hour, or minute when I will not miss him.

But if I know Bill, he'll keep letting me know he's all right.

EPILOGUE

I don't need my ears to hear your song.

The Final Measure

Five months have passed since Bill died.

It feels like yesterday. It feels like a hundred years ago.

He is gone.

In the time since his death, I have been hospitalized twice: once to have my infected chest catheter removed, and once to have a new one inserted. The infection caused me to experience the "shake and bake" episodes I had previously only witnessed in Bill. I dropped to one hundred three pounds, mostly due to persistent diarrhea and little interest in eating alone. The *M. haemophilum* came out of remission as a leg nodule that has remained active since early December. Henry's tactic now is to go directly after the HIV and try to give my immune system a fighting chance to help itself. I started a new experimental drug last week as part of this plan.

Neither my hearing nor my eyesight has deteriorated any further. I have a T-cell count of seventy-seven, which should make me happy, particularly when I remember that, at the time of his death, Bill's count was around five.

I am not happy. I am not unhappy.

Right now, I just am.

It is the lack of feeling that is so strange. After years of such intense involvement with Bill, uninvolvement feels foreign, unnatural. Bill gave me a purpose. Even when all I did was sit by his bedside, I had a purpose: to let him know I loved him. Visiting him at the hospital gave me a reason to get up every day. Taking care of him, keeping him comfortable, helping him feel independent—these activities gave me a purpose.

When Bill died, I lost that purpose. Suddenly my identity as half of a cherished whole disintegrated.

Every night since the twenty-second of August I have dreamed of Bill. For the first month I had nightmares in which Bill was dead. And he was always dead because I had made the wrong decision. In some nightmares I gave permission for surgery that killed him; in others I didn't give permission for surgery that could have saved him. Once I dreamed that I mistakenly pulled out his nasogastric tube and caused him to drown in his own fluids. My actions had deadly consequences.

A few weeks later my dreams changed. Bill was alive, although it was clear he was dying. We did the same things in my dreams that we had done in reality, and, as in reality, they ended with Bill's suffering and death. But I had stopped feeling so responsible for the events that unfolded. Bill was now a decision-maker, where before he had just been a passive victim of my misministrations.

My most recent dreams no longer frighten me; they are not nightmares. In them, Bill and I talk naturally about mundane, normal things. We make plans, we take trips, we eat together. We act as if neither one of us ever had AIDS. In these dreams I am again one half of a lovely whole.

Sometimes I am tempted not to wake up.

I am in mourning.

I don't know how to be an adult without Bill. We married so young that in many ways we grew up together. At thirty-one, I now must find the person Bill left behind.

I'm not sure yet whether I will like her when I find her.

Soon after Bill's death I went on a shopping frenzy. None of my clothes fit anymore; I had gone from a size ten to a size five in less than a year. But even if I were still a size ten, even if my clothes weren't so baggy, they wouldn't fit.

They are from that other life. They belong to that other person, and she is gone.

I try new makeup; I try new styles. I try to reconstruct the person I was before Bill came into my life. I never feel quite together; styles have changed. I still brush color onto my cheeks and my lips and my eyelids; I carefully fill in the lines of me that Bill once filled. If I keep coloring myself in, I think, then perhaps a picture will emerge, perhaps one day I'll gaze in the mirror and say, "*There* you are! I've been looking all over for you!"

I try to create the thirty-one-year-old of my dreams, a woman attractive and desirable, a woman tinted with life. But now I know that dreams rarely come true. I now know that the truth always surfaces.

Some widows might be tempted to reenter the mainstream, look for another man. Can you imagine my personal ad?

Single, white, HIV+ female, two hearing aids, failing eyes, underweight, less than one-hundred T cells, Porta-cath, widespread scarring, thinning hair, numb feet. Seeks man who should know better for possibly short-term relationship. Must be able to look death in the eye.

Not an easy sell. Not exactly the kind of girl you'd bring home to Mother.

If I were a normal widow, I'd grieve and know I might love again. If I were a widow with another terminal illness—cancer, maybe—I'd mourn and hope to find someone to embrace both me and my malignancy. But I am a widow with AIDS. I am toxic; I could kill.

This is the cruelest side effect of AIDS: it makes its victims feel unlovable.

AIDS killed the greatest love in my life. AIDS killed the person who found me lovable despite the unlovable disease we shared. AIDS continues to kill my hope for love in the future.

But I had a love whose music soared beyond sound. I had a love, despite AIDS.

Sometimes I wonder why I try so hard when I know that no infusion, no pill, no word on paper will save me. After Bill died, I felt unnecessary, superfluous. I became paranoid. I thought everyone just humored me and my desire to live, and waited for me to die, because dying was the only thing now left for me to do. I assumed everyone thought I was worthless without Bill.

I think I am the only one who actually felt that way.

I rationalized just to get through each day, until I no longer needed to fool myself into thinking I wanted to live. On some days, dark days, I still feel it would make for a better story if I killed myself or died of grief.

But those are rare days. Most days I continue doing the work Bill and I started. I think about my next book; I attend a weekly writing workshop. I plan a springtime trip to New Orleans with my sisters.

I recently returned to playing the piano after being away from it for almost two years. My hearing aids cannot make music sound tuneful; they simply amplify the sounds I am able to hear, sounds still more often distorted than not. Although music still sounds strange, I have become somewhat used to the strangeness. I was surprised to discover that perhaps not all of the music is gone from my life.

I was surprised to learn that I want to live. I was surprised to look in the mirror one morning and find that I wasn't unhappy with the person who looked back.

There you are.

Two weeks after Bill's death I received a package in the mail. It was a collection of CDs that Bill had ordered for me from his hospital bed, the birthday present he couldn't get to a store to buy. They contained music from the 1970s, pre-AIDS music, music he knew I could enjoy because my memory would sing the melodies.

I can hear the music he gave me.

It is the most romantic gift I've ever received. It was Bill's way of saying, "I'll try to put some music back into your life. I'll try to fill in the parts you have lost."

I love you, he said.

I had a love, despite AIDS.

I could live off this love for the rest of my life.

I think I will.

The song that started eleven years ago has reached its final measures. It is now up to me to make sure they are beautifully played.

By the year 2000, 2 out of 3 Americans could be illiterate.

It's true.

Today, 75 million adults… about one American in three can't read adequately. And by the year 2000, U.S. News & World Report envisions an America with a literacy rate of only 30%.

Before that America comes to be, you can stop it… by joining the fight against illiteracy today.

Call the Coalition for Literacy at toll-free **1-800-228-8813** and volunteer.

Volunteer Against Illiteracy. The only degree you need is a degree of caring.

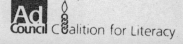

Ad Council Coalition for Literacy